JENNIFER CLARKE was l
both her parents taught. Sh
Dramatic Art in London and worked as an actress for several
years. Later she lived in Scotland and then in Wales where she
taught drama at Dyfed College of Art in Carmarthen. Returning
to London, she became a registered London Tourist Board guide.
She now works in the publicity department of the Barbican
Centre. She loves to walk, swim, read and travel, and has one
daughter who is an artist.

JOANNA PARKIN was born in Swansea in 1938, and from
1955–57 studied photography at the Regent Street Polytechnic.
She then spent two years as a staff photographer for the *Slough
Observer*. Since 1961 she has worked as a freelance photographer
for various national newspapers and magazines. She now lives in
Hampton Hill, Middlesex with her husband and three children,
and describes her greatest treat as their holidays in Scotland, as
far away as possible from people and traffic.

Jennifer Clarke and Joanna Parkin are sisters and have
collaborated on another book in this series, *In Our
Grandmother's Footsteps: A Virago Guide to London.*

Exploring the
WEST COUNTRY
A Woman's Guide

JENNIFER CLARKE

Photographs by Joanna Parkin

Published by VIRAGO PRESS Limited 1987
41 William IV Street, London WC2N 4DB

Text copyright © Jennifer Clarke 1987

Illustrations copyright for her photographs
© Joanna Parkin 1987

British Library Cataloguing in Publication Data
Clarke, Jennifer
 Exploring the West country.
  1. West Country (England) – Description
  and travel – Guide-books
  I. Title II. Parkin, Joanna
  914.23'04858   DA670.W49
  ISBN 0-86068-601-9

Photoset by Rowland Phototypesetting Ltd
Bury St Edmunds, Suffolk
Printed in Great Britain by Anchor Brendon Ltd
of Tiptree, Essex

This book is dedicated to
Elizabeth Beckett, Diana Frayne, Cecilia Jenkins,
Bobby Macer, Mary Smith,
and all the others who made us so comfortable
and fed us so royally on our travels.

ACKNOWLEDGEMENTS

We would like to acknowledge the debt we owe to the staff of all
the libraries, museums and art galleries, and to all the archivists,
who answered our endless questions and letters with a generosity
that was overwhelming.

For other particular help we would like to thank Rebecca
Alderwick, Assistant Press Officer, National Federation of
Women's Institutes; *Andrews* of Teddington; Camilla Bagg; The
Revd R. Bagott; Martin Val Baker, *The Peninsula Voice*,
Penzance; Kate Baker; The Revd Peter Brightman; Mary
Campbell; Margaret Church; Caroline and George Cornish;
Susan Cox, The English Lace School; Margaret Crews; Pat
Davies, The London Symphony Chorus; Peter Dadd, The Othona
Community; The Revd A. Dick; Christopher Driver; Barbara
Entwistle; Christine Gilson; The Revd F. L. R. Graham; Joy Foot,
Cornwall Federation of Women's Institutes; Mrs Margery Kelly;
The Revd Canon Philip Maddock; Anthony Mitchell, The
National Trust; Marilyn Morris; Oliver Padel; Stanley D. Parkin;
Roy Soper; Mrs Spiers, The Tamar Protection Society; Anne
Stanford; Linda Taylor; The Revd Bryan Thomas; Derek Toyne;
The Revd David Webb; Anne Welsford; Mary Williams; Mrs
G. M. Weall; Mrs C. Williams; Mrs Hilary Wrench and John
Yallop.

Once again we wish to thank our father, Waldo Clarke, for his
constant encouragement and invaluable help.

The photographs listed below are reproduced by kind permission
of the following: Abson Books, Bristol, p. 23; Barbara Hepworth
Museum, St Ives, p. 48; British Library, London, p. 118;
reproduced by courtesy of the trustees of the British Museum,
London, p. 16; City of Bristol Museum and Art Gallery, Bristol,
p. 30; Devon Library Services, p. 83; English China Clays
Groups, St Austell, p. 35; Cyril Stanborough, p. 144.

CONTENTS

This book is arranged alphabetically by county, and alphabetically by the women who are its subjects within each county. The index at the end will help you to locate the entry for each subject.

PREFACE

We set off to explore the West Country, in search of the women who had links with the area, with some trepidation. Our first book about women of London had presented few problems in terms of material – if anything, there was too much! But Avon, Cornwall, Devon, Dorset, Somerset and Wiltshire were a different matter. It was reasonable to expect major cities such as Bath and Exeter to provide good hunting grounds, but in the rural areas, the villages, the country churches, the small seaside towns, would we find the evidence we were looking for? Would we find the memorials, the plaques, graves and statues that would lead us to the lives of the women of the West Country?

We need not have worried. Slowly at first, then more impatiently, women began to jostle for our attention. They had carved wood, written poetry, made lace, become champion rowers and walked two hundred miles. They had left treasured property to the nation, founded schools, sold fish and worked in the mines. Some had been murdered, others had committed murder. As always, some categories dominated: women saints and women painters proliferated and had to be severely pruned.

Once again we have only skimmed the surface, and many women have had to be left out. (For example, we have not included Mary Wollstonecraft and Mary Shelley who are both buried in St Peter's churchyard, Bournemouth. Their burial there, however, is their only link with Dorset.) Those whose footsteps we have traced lived rich, rare and immensely varied lives. To our great delight we came across several examples of their work, and have included photographs of these wherever possible.

During the two years we spent exploring some of the most beautiful countryside in Britain, we met many women who live and work there now. Without their generous help, encouragement and hospitality this book could not have been written.

The West Country

0   10   20 Miles
0   10   20   30 Kilometres

Ilfracombe ○

○ Bar

○ Bideford

ATLANTIC OCEAN

Bude ○

DEV

Okehampton ○

Camelford ○

Launceston ○

DART.

CORNWALL

○ Tavistock

○ Bodmin

Saltash ○

T

Fowey ○

○ Plymouth

Devonport ○

St. Ives ○

Redruth ○

○ Truro

Lands ○
End

○ Penzance

Helston ○

○ Falmouth

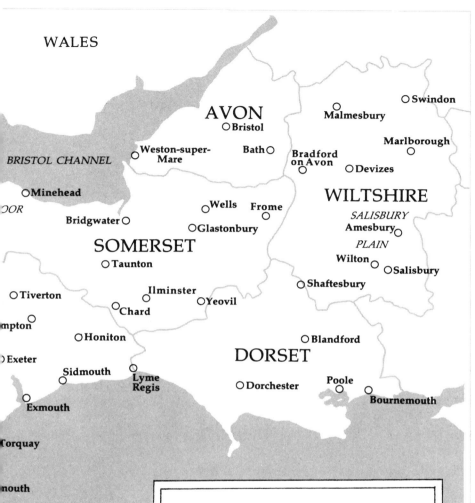

WALES

AVON

○ Swindon

Malmesbury

○ Bristol

BRISTOL CHANNEL

○ Weston-super-
Mare

Bath ○

Marlborough
○

Bradford
on Avon
○

○ Devizes

○ Minehead

DOR

Bridgwater ○

○ Wells   Frome
○

○ Glastonbury

WILTSHIRE

SALISBURY

Amesbury ○

SOMERSET

○ Taunton

PLAIN

Wilton ○

○ Salisbury

○ Tiverton

Ilminster
○

○ Chard

○ Yeovil

○ Shaftesbury

mpton ○

○ Honiton

○ Blandford

○ Exeter

DORSET

Sidmouth
○

Lyme
Regis ○

○ Dorchester

Poole
○ ○

○
Exmouth

Bournemouth

orquay

nouth

This map shows the cities and main towns
referred to in *Exploring the West Country*. For
further reference, there is a wide range of maps
available on the area: the National Map series,
particularly recommended for motorists; the
Leisure Map series, specially designed for the
sightseer; the Ordnance Survey Holiday Map and
Guide of the West Country, and for people
planning to explore an area in greater detail: the
range of 1:25000 and 1:50000 Ordnance Survey
Maps.

AVON

JANE AUSTEN
1775–1817
Plaque: 4 Sydney Place, Bath

Jane Austen scarcely needs an introduction. Born at Steventon in Hampshire, she wrote only six novels and died at Winchester aged forty-two. In his diary, Sir Walter Scott wrote:

> I read and for the third time Miss Austen's very finely written novel of Pride and Prejudice. That young lady had a talent for describing the feelings, characters, and

4 Sydney Place, Bath, home of Jane Austen

involvements of ordinary life the most wonderful I ever met with. The big wow-wow I can do myself like any one going, but the exquisite touch which renders common-place things and characters interesting from the truth and description of the sentiment is denied to me. What a pity that so gifted a creature died so early!

In 1801 Jane's father, the Reverend George Austen, retired from his living at Steventon and moved his family to Bath. He died in 1805 and, a year later, Jane, her mother and her sister, Cassandra, moved away to Clifton, Southampton and finally Chawton, in Hampshire.
Jane was in her mid-twenties when she lived in Bath. She used it as a background in two of her novels, *Northanger Abbey* and *Persuasion*, but one feels that she was not particularly fond of the city. Indeed, she once wrote to her sister: 'It will be two years tomorrow since we left Bath for Clifton, with what happy feelings of escape!'
A bronze plaque on 4 Sydney Place identifies it as Jane's 'principal domicile' in Bath, but she also lived at 27 Green Park Buildings and 25 Gay Street.

MARY BAKER (PRINCESS CARABOO)
1792–1864
(née Wilcocks)
Almondsbury near Bristol

Oh! young Caraboo is come out of the west,
In Frenchified tatters the damsel is dressed
And, save one pair of worsted, she stockings had none,
She tramped half unshod, and she walked all alone:
But how to bamboozle the doxy well knew;
'You ne'er heard of a gypsy like young Caraboo.
(Anon., *Caraboo. A Narrative of a Singular Imposition*, 1817)

On 3 April 1817, at Almondsbury near Bristol, Mr Samuel Warrall, a magistrate, and his wife were disturbed by someone knocking at their door. It was the overseer of the parish. He had come to inform them that a young woman, dressed in most unusual and exotic clothes, had arrived at a cottage in the village. Using signs (she did not seem to speak English), she had asked to be allowed to sleep there.
Mr and Mrs Warrall offered to

Portrait of Mary Baker,
alias Princess Caraboo

take in this mysterious foreigner. Gradually over the next few months the language barrier was broken down and the Warralls learnt that for her a knife was *savoo*, *vellee* was a bed, *raglish*, a woman and *alla tulla*, God. Her father, they gathered, was Chinese, her mother had come from Batavia – she herself was the Princess of Javasu. How or why she had arrived at Almondsbury she was unable to explain. Meanwhile people came from far and wide to meet their unusual and interesting guest.

There was only one determined sceptic, a Dr Wilkinson of Bath. He made exhaustive enquiries and discovered that the so-called Princess of Javasu was really Mary Baker, the daughter of Thomas Wilcocks, a shoe maker of Witheridge in Devon. When faced with the evidence, she admitted everything, asking only that her parents should not be involved.

Mary, it seems, was always a rebel. She had hated school and

occupied much of her time fishing, swimming or playing bowls. At sixteen she was employed as a domestic servant, but spent most of her money buying clothes. This extravagance may have caused the bitter quarrel between Mary and her father, which resulted in him giving her a beating. She promptly left home for good and went to London, where she met, and probably married, a Mr Bakerstendt, or Bickerstein. It was at this time that she picked up an extensive knowledge of an Asian language, possibly Malayan. Mary then parted from Mr Bakerstendt and moved to Bristol, where she lived for a while with a young woman called Eleanor Josephs. Then, one evening in 1817, she turned up at Almondsbury and knocked on a cottage door.

Mary's brilliant hoax resulted in some very red faces. She was packed off to America where she lived in Philadelphia under the assumed name of Mary Burgess. About thirty years later she returned to England and earned a rather precarious living by selling and applying leeches. She died in Bristol.

But what shall be said of all the learned travellers, the philosophers, the cognoscenti, the blue stocking ladies, and the numerous dupes of various denominations, who were so completely juggled and out-witted? – They must console themselves with the doctrine of Hudibras,
   That the pleasure is as great
   In being *cheated*, as to cheat.
(Anon., *Caraboo. A Narrative of a Singular Imposition*, 1817)

JANE
BOWDLER
1743–1784

HENRIETTA
BOWDLER
1754–1830
Lived: Bath

Jane and Henrietta Bowdler both lived and died in Bath. One of their brothers, Thomas, edited a *Family Shakespeare*, from which he had carefully removed anything he considered unsuitable for family reading.

Jane, the elder sister, was never strong and became a confirmed invalid after an attack of smallpox in 1759. She wrote many poems

and essays which were published after her death. Any profits were to benefit the hospital at Bath. The hospital must have done quite well as, although the contents were not particularly exciting, the book was remarkably successful and, between 1787 and 1830, ran into sixteen editions.

Henrietta's *Poems and Essays* was published in 1786. She was a

FRANCES (FANNY) BURNEY

1752–1840
(Madame D'Arblay)
Buried: Walcot Parish
Church, Bath

deeply religious woman and when Bishop Porteous of London read her 'Sermons on the Doctrines and Duties of Christianity', he assumed the anonymous author to be a man and wrote to offer him a living. She would not allow her romantic

novel, *Pen Tamar; or the History of an Old Maid*, to be published until after her death. This led to speculation that it was semi-autobiographical; it was even more popular than her sister's book and ran to *fifty* editions.

The two graveyards on either side of Walcot Parish Church, Bath, have been almost entirely cleared of tombs and gravestones. However, in the middle of the smaller lawn, in solitary splendour, stands the tomb of Fanny Burney, novelist and diarist. She was buried there, with her husband and her son, both of whom had predeceased her.

Fanny became a celebrity in 1778, when it was discovered that she was the anonymous author of a

popular novel called *Evelina*. She later published *Cecilia* (1782), *Camilla* (1796) and *The Wanderer* (1814). She knew Dr Johnson and was also a close friend of Mrs Thrale.

Fanny's lively *Diary and Letters* was published after her death, the first five volumes appearing in 1842. Her visit to Bath in 1780 is well recorded and includes several rather waspish descriptions of local celebrities, including Lady Anna Miller (q.v.).

Fanny Burney's tomb at
Walcot Parish Church,
Bath

MARY CARPENTER

1807–1877
Memorial: Bristol
Cathedral

Mary Carpenter, one of the greatest pioneers of social reform in nineteenth-century England, became famous as the founder of the first Reformatory for Girls at Bristol, in 1854.

Born at Exeter in Devon, she was the daughter of the Reverend Lant Carpenter and his wife, Anna, dedicated Nonconformists and Unitarians. When Mary was ten years old, the family moved to Bristol (where her father became minister at Lewin's Mead) and lived in Great George Street. Mary attended her father's school and developed into an introspective, religious and serious young woman.

In 1831 Mary was made Superintendent of the Lewin's Mead Sunday School and came face to face with the effects of poverty and ignorance. Nine years later, after her father's death, she helped her mother to run a school for girls, but this was not enough of a challenge and she began to collect money for a project closer to her own heart. In 1846 she opened a 'Ragged School'.

> Mary Carpenter was well aware that many of her pupils were thieves. They worked in gangs, the Lewin's Mead Gang, the St James' Back Gang, the Milk Street Gang, and so on . . . The casual brutality of prison life, in her observation, did these children nothing but harm. (Jo Manton, *Mary Carpenter and the Children of the Streets*, 1976)

In 1850 she published *Ragged Schools* and, in 1851, *Reformatory Schools for the Children of the Perishing and Dangerous Classes*. In 1854 a Reformatory School for girls was opened in a house known as Red Lodge in Park Row, Bristol. Mary Carpenter was Lady Superintendent until her death, over twenty years later. It was often disappointing work and Mary's patience was sometimes stretched to breaking point. Staff occasionally proved incompetent and had to be dismissed. The girls, always unpredictable, seemed at times quite beyond redemption and had to be sent away to the colonies. Nevertheless the experiment continued and foundations were laid for the future.

Mary Carpenter had other interests. She visited India several times, paying particular attention to the improvement of education for Indian women. She founded girls' schools at both Bombay and Ahmedabad, paying the costs for their first year of existence out of her own funds.

After her death, in 1877, a memorial was placed in Bristol Cathedral. The inscription includes these words:

> No human ill escaped her pity nor cast down her trust: with true self sacrifice she followed in the train of Christ, to seek and to save that which was lost and bring it home to the Father in heaven.

SACRED TO THE MEMORY OF

MARY CARPENTER

SUSANNAH DOBSON

d. 1795
(née Dawson)
Lived: Bath

Though coarse, low-bred, forward, self-sufficient, and flaunting, she seems to have a strong and masculine understanding, and parts that, had they been united with modesty, or fostered by education, might have made her a shining and agreeable woman; but she has evidently kept low company, which she has risen above in literature, but not in manners. (Fanny Burney, *Diary and Letters of Madame D'Arblay*, 1842–6)

Very little is known about Susannah Dobson, but Fanny Burney (q.v.) met her (and obviously disliked her) in Bath. Her unfavourable description only seems to make Susannah more interesting.

Susannah was married to a doctor, Matthew Dobson, who came from Liverpool. She was an intelligent woman and a translator of great ability. Her *Life of Petrarch*, translated from de Sade's *Mémoires pour la vie de Petrarch*, was first published in 1775. Four years later, she translated Sainte-Palaye's *Literary History of the Troubadours*.

Dr Dobson died in Bath in 1784; Susannah died eleven years later. She was buried at St Paul's Church, Covent Garden, in London.

MARY ELIZABETH DUFFIELD

1819–1914
(née Rosenberg)
Lived: Bath

The principles of Art are universal, and applicable to every kind of composition; the same harmonious arrangement, which gives a beauty never yet surpassed to the works of Rubens and Titian, is equally desirable in the smallest and most insignificant group of flowers. (Mrs Duffield, *The Art of Flower Painting*, 1856)

Mary's father, Thomas Rosenberg, was well-known in Bath as an artist and teacher, and all five of his children followed in his footsteps. Mary, from an early age, chose to specialize in flower painting and in 1834, aged only fifteen, she won a silver medal from the Society of Arts.

In 1850 she married William Duffield, also a painter and also a native of Bath. She had two children, continued to work and, in 1856, Winsor and Newton published her *Art of Flower Painting*, with twelve illustrations on wood, engraved by Dalziel.

Mary was elected a member of the New Water Colour Society in 1861. Two years later her husband died from what was thought to be an infection caused by the decaying body of a stag, left for too long in his studio.

Mary Elizabeth Duffield eventually settled in Hythe, Kent, and lived to the grand old age of ninety-five.

AMELIA EDWARDS

1831–1892
Buried: Henbury Parish Church

At Henbury, on the outskirts of Bristol, is a small but interesting parish church and, in the churchyard there, tucked against the church wall, is a most unusual grave. A large, white marble *Ankh* (the ancient Egyptian symbol of enduring life and generative energy) lies flat on the slab and, at the head, there is a marble obelisk. It is the grave of Amelia Edwards.

Amelia was born in London and educated at home. She enjoyed drawing, music and particularly writing, but it was a casual switch of plan in a holiday itinerary that completely changed her life. She visited Egypt in 1873 and was irrevocably 'hooked'.

Realizing that the antiquities in Egypt were being slowly but surely destroyed, Amelia decided that there was only one remedy – scientific excavation. She threw every ounce of her energy into an attempt to preserve Ancient Egypt for posterity. In 1877 her book, *A Thousand Miles Up the Nile*, was published. In 1882 she helped to found the Egypt Exploration Fund and devoted the rest of her life to this cause.

Amelia retired to Westbury-on-Trym, near Bristol. She died at Weston-Super-Mare and was buried at Henbury, leaving her library and collection of Egyptian antiquities to University College, London. She also left enough money to establish a Chair of Egyptology – the first in Britain.

Amelia Edwards's grave at Henbury Parish Church

SARAH FIELDING

1710–1768
Plaque: Bath Abbey

Sarah Fielding's novel, *The Adventures of David Simple: Containing an Account of his Travels in the Search of a Real Friend*, first appeared in 1744. Her well-known brother, Henry

Fielding (the author of *Tom Jones*), wrote the preface. As certain doubts had been voiced, most of his introduction was devoted to a fierce insistence on his sister's sole authorship: 'Indeed I believe there are few books in the world so absolutely the author's own as this.'

Sarah, born in Dorset, eventually settled in Bath. An intelligent and talented writer, she produced not only *David Simple* and a sequel, but also a novel called *The Governess* in 1749. Her patron was the postal reformer and entrepreneur of Bath, Ralph Allen, who is said to have given her a pension of a hundred pounds for the pleasure her writing gave him. She lived for a while at Widcombe Lodge in Bath, and when she died she was buried at Charlcombe.

In the Abbey Church at Bath there is a plaque to Sarah Fielding tucked away in a dark corner to the left of the main entrance.

SARAH GRAND (MRS FRANCES ELIZABETH McFALL)

1854–1943
(Née Clarke)
Lived: Sion Hill Place, Bath

Frances Clarke was born in Ireland, but, when she was seven, her father died and the family moved to Yorkshire. In 1870 she married Surgeon-Major David McFall, a thirty-nine year old widower (she later remarked that she had married at sixteen to escape from school). Frances travelled to China and Japan with her husband, gave birth to a son, and began to write, using the pseudonym Sarah Grand.

Her first modest success, *Ideala*, was published in 1888. Then she made a decision that in those days was astounding. She left her husband and son. Five years later her novel *The Heavenly Twins* became a best-seller. In 1897 her next novel, *The Beth Book*, was published:

> Sarah Grand's *The Beth Book* . . . is one of our few nineteenth-century

portraits of the artist as a young woman, 'a study from the life' of a 'woman of genius' who overcomes a deprived childhood and an oppressive marriage to become a distinguished writer and a great feminist orator. (*The Beth Book*: new introduction to Virago 1980 edition)

After her husband's death in 1898, Mrs McFall became involved in the suffrage campaign. A member of the Women Writers' Suffrage League, she also became President of the National Union of Women's Suffrage Societies in Tunbridge Wells, Kent, where she was living at the time. In 1920 she moved to Bath and two years later became Mayoress there, a position she held for six years. Mrs McFall – Sarah Grand – slipped quietly into obscurity and died at Calne, in Wiltshire, aged eighty-nine.

SARAH ANN HENLEY

1863–1948
(Mrs Lane)
Clifton Suspension Bridge

EXTRAORDINARY LEAP FROM THE SUSPENSION BRIDGE

Yesterday, at a little past mid-day, Sarah Ann Henley, of 48 Twinnell Road, St Philip's, leaped from the Suspension Bridge, and, singular to state, when picked up in the mud below was conscious, and very soon after was able to state her name and address. The person who had such a marvellous escape is a young woman, 22 years of age, living with her father, a respectable working man, at the above address. (*The Western Daily Press*, 9 May 1885)

Sarah Ann Henley had thrown herself off the Clifton Suspension Bridge, Bristol, fell about two hundred and fifty feet – and survived.

A barmaid at the Rising Sun at Ashton, Sarah had been going out with a young man who worked as a porter on the Great Western Railway. On Thursday 7 May 1885, she received a letter from him ending their relationship. Several neighbours noticed that she seemed extremely depressed and the following day she walked to the bridge and made her terrifying leap. The *Bristol Magpie*, on 16 May, gave this explanation for her amazing escape from what should have been certain death:

> There being a slight breeze blowing on Friday, the young woman's clothes were inflated and her descent was thereby considerably checked; and the wind also prevented her falling straight into the water, and she was carried into the mud on the Gloucestershire side.

Sarah soon recovered from her frightful ordeal and, a few years later, married not her porter but a Mr Edward Lane. She lived to the age of eighty-five and was buried in Avon View Cemetery. She has become one of the legends of the Suspension Bridge.

VICTORIA HUGHES

1897–1978
Durdham Downs, Bristol

I swallowed my pride and became a 'loo lady' on a Thursday afternoon in the summer of 1929.

From this first sentence, to the end of the book, Victoria Hughes' *Ladies' Mile* (1977) is addictive reading. Sensitively edited by David Foot, it tells the story of Victoria's life as a cloakroom attendant in Bristol. She spent thirty-three years looking after ladies' toilets, particularly the one on Durdham Downs, close to the notorious 'Ladies' Mile':

> It appeared to me that nearly all the tarts in Bristol used to meet at the lavatory on the Downs. My early impressions of the place left me in no doubt at all.

Victoria Hughes talked to the prostitutes who patrolled the area and made them cups of tea. Sometimes she was appalled, sometimes sympathetic – and occasionally she was terrified, particularly of the men she called the 'lurkers'. Not once, in all those years, was she bored.

She retired in 1962 and her book was published fifteen years later, when she was eighty. She thoroughly enjoyed all the publicity and television interviews, and has been described by her publishers as a dear and most appreciative author. She died the year after publication.

Victoria Hughes was born in Bristol; life was not easy and the family was poor. When Victoria left school she went to work in a tobacco factory and met the man who was to become her husband, Richard Hughes. They were married in 1916, during the First World War, when he was called up and told that he was to be sent to France. On his return they managed to find a flat and started to make a life together. But, after a while, things began to go wrong. Richard's eyesight was deteriorating, their first daughter, Margaret, had feeding problems and, perhaps worst of all, unemployment was increasing at a frightening rate.

Victoria tried nursing but, with a

Victoria Hughes

toddler to take care of, was forced to give up. She worked as a nanny for three months – and saved two pounds. She was beginning to despair:

It was about this time when I was returning sadly from an unsuccessful

job application that I went to spend a penny. I entered the public toilet and my coin got wedged. The attendant kindly opened the door for me, heard how hard I'd been trying to get work and started me on a new career.

SOPHIA LEE
1750–1824
HARRIET LEE
1757–1851
Buried: St Andrew's
Church, Clifton
(now demolished)

Sophia and Harriet were the daughters of John Lee, a London actor, and both became writers. When their father died they moved to Bath where they opened a school at Belvedere House.

Sophia's three-act opera, *The Chapter of Accidents*, based on Diderot's *Père de Famille* was produced in 1780 as a five-act comedy at the Haymarket Theatre, London. She also wrote one of the earliest historical romances published in England, *The Recess, or a Tale of other Times* (1785).

Harriet published a novel, *The Errors of Innocence*, in 1786, and

her comedy *The New Peerage, or our Eyes may deceive us* was performed at Drury Lane, London, a year later.

The sisters' best known work, *The Canterbury Tales* (1797–1805) was a joint effort and very popular at the time. They retired to Bristol and lived at Clifton, where Harriet later met another pair of literary sisters, Jane and Anna Maria Porter (q.v.).

Sophia and Harriet were both buried in St Andrew's, Clifton. The church was later bombed and then demolished.

ELIZABETH LINLEY

1754–1792
(Mrs Sheridan)
Plaque: 11 Royal
Crescent, Bath

At 11 Royal Crescent, Bath, there is a plaque that reads:

Thomas Linley lived here and from this house his daughter Elizabeth eloped with Richard Brinsley Sheridan on the evening of the 18th March 1772.

The Linleys were an exceptionally accomplished family: Elizabeth's father was a composer, her brother was a talented violinist, and both she and her sister Mary sang. Elizabeth performed at concerts arranged by her father at Bath, Bristol, Oxford and other venues. She was also exceptionally beautiful. Fanny Burney (q.v.), who rarely flattered anyone, described her:

Her complexion a clear, lovely, animated brown, with a bloomy colour on her cheeks, her nose that most elegant of shapes, Grecian; fine, luxurious easy-sitting hair, a charming forehead, pretty mouth and most beautiful eyes. (Fanny Burney, *Diary and Letters of Madame D'Arblay*, 1842–46)

Elizabeth attracted a large number of admirers, among them an unpleasant man, Captain Mathews, who was already married. Elizabeth, in an attempt to avoid his unwelcome attentions, turned to a young – and handsome – friend of the family, Richard Brinsley Sheridan. Without telling her father, Sheridan offered to act as her escort when she fled to France. He accompanied her across the Channel and went through a form of marriage in

Calais to protect her reputation. Elizabeth's father caught up with them in Lille and they were separated.

Almost a year later, after two duels between Sheridan and Mathews and much emotional confrontation between their respective families, Elizabeth and Richard were properly married at Marylebone Church in London. The couple settled in London. Richard, brilliant, charismatic and slightly unstable, became the manager of Drury Lane Theatre. He wrote a few highly successful plays, notably *The Rivals, The School for Scandal* and *The Critic* and in 1780 entered Parliament as Member for Stafford.

Elizabeth gave up singing in public after her marriage. She gave birth to a son and helped her husband by keeping accounts and reading manuscripts. In spite of Richard's unreliability and his infidelity – which made her desperately unhappy – she understood him and loved him dearly. Once, when answering a letter from him, announcing some success on the political front, she ended her reply with these words:

God bless thee, my dear soul. Thank ye for the good news of politics. I hope it all really good but ye are such a sanguine pig, there's no knowing.

Elizabeth was only thirty-eight when she died of consumption at Hot Wells, Bristol. She was buried at Wells, in Somerset.

11 Royal Crescent, Bath
from where Elizabeth
Linley eloped

SALLY LUNN

c. 1680?
North Parade Passage, Bath

In North Parade Passage, Bath, there is a picturesque old house, said to have been built for the Duke of Kingston in the fifteenth century. For many years it has been a tea shop, known as 'Sally Lunn's'.

Some people say that Sally is only a legend. Admittedly there seem to be no solid facts to substantiate her existence, apart from the discovery long ago, in the cellar of the house, of some recipes for tea cakes. Nevertheless Sally's name is solidly entrenched in local history, and one can only hope that there *was* a Sally Lunn, who baked delicious tea cakes and once sold them round the streets of Bath.

Sally Lunn's House,
North Parade Passage,
Bath

EMMA MARSHALL

1830–1899
(née Martin)
Plaque: Bristol Cathedral

Born at Cromer, in Norfolk, Emma Martin moved to Clifton, Bristol, where she later married Mr Marshall, a bank clerk. She had seven children and, after living in Somerset, Devon and Gloucestershire, eventually returned to Bristol. She wrote many novels, the most popular being a historical romance, *In Colston's Days* (1884), which was set in seventeenth-century Bristol:

The sun was setting in a sky which was painted with every shade of amethyst and gold, ethereal green, and tenderest sapphire, melting into opal tints of indescribable loveliness.

A few detached clouds floated over the old city of Bristol, sent as messengers from the sunset; their snowy breasts were tinged with bright crimson, and reflected a ruddy glow upon the dull waters of the Avon, flowing swiftly out under the arches of the bridge, seaward.

After her death, in 1899, a memorial plaque was placed in Bristol Cathedral.

LADY ANNA MILLER

1741–1781
(née Riggs)
Monument: Bath Abbey

Nothing is more tonish than to visit Lady Miller. She is a round, plump, coarse-looking dame of about forty, and while all her aim is to appear an elegant woman of fashion, all her success is to seem an ordinary woman in very common life, with fine clothes on. Her habits are bustling, her air is mock-important, and her manners very inelegant. (*Diary and Letters of Madame D'Arblay*, 1842–46)

One assumes that Madame D'Arblay (Fanny Burney, q.v.), did not think much of Lady Miller, who had become one of the most fashionable literary hostesses in Bath by the late eighteenth century.

Married in 1765, Lady Miller visited Italy with her husband, and returned with a large Tuscan vase and a taste for poetry. She then published, anonymously, *Letters from Italy, Describing the Manners, Customs, Antiquities, Paintings* (1776). At her home, Batheaston Villa, she held parties and invited the intelligentsia, the aristocratic and the successful. The highlight of these gatherings was a competition. Guests were encouraged to write poetry – either on a subject suggested by their hostess, or the composition of *Bouts Rimés*, very short poems organized around specific patterns – which they then placed in Lady Miller's *Frascati* vase. The poems were drawn from the vase and read aloud – and the authors of the first three poems voted the best were ceremoniously crowned with myrtle. Many mocked, but Lady Miller's soirées were extremely popular. It was not unusual to see up to fifty carriages waiting outside her house.

The excitement was obviously too much for her and she died in 1781. *The Gentleman's Magazine* gave her one of their inimitable obituaries:

> Suddenly, at Bristol Hot Wells, Lady Miller, author of *Letters from Italy* . . . and other more glorious works of charity, humanity and goodness, which will remain more durable monuments of her virtues, and of her loss. Her ladyship died about the middle period of her life, in her chair, and without a groan.

She was buried in the Abbey at Bath, and in 1785 a monument to her memory was placed there, to the left of the altar.

Monument of Lady Anna Miller in Bath Abbey

HANNAH MORE

1745–1833

Buried: All Saints Church, Wrington (a bust in church porch)

Bust of Hannah More in the garden of Barley Wood House, Wrington (not open to visitors)

I sometimes say there are 98 reasons for living in the country and but two for living in a town. I will spare you the 98, but the two are – the churches are damp, and if you want to see a book you must buy it, for you can neither hire nor borrow. (Hannah More to J. S. Duncan, Esq)

In September 1983 a 'Hannah More Week' was held in the village of Wrington near Bristol. The celebrations included a commemorative service, an exhibition of letters and writings of Hannah More and other historical items and an evening of dramatic readings and musical interludes in Wrington Memorial Hall.

Hannah was born in Fishponds, Bristol. Her father was a schoolmaster and he educated his five daughters so well that, when they grew up, they established a school for 'young ladies' in Park Street. For a while Hannah was

romantically involved with a Mr Turner, who was almost twice her age. When their engagement was broken off Mr Turner nobly insisted on giving her an annuity and she was able to make her dream of 'riding to London to see bishops and booksellers' come true.

In London Hannah sparkled. She knew Frances Reynolds (q.v.), the sister of Sir Joshua, and through her met many celebrities, among them the actor David Garrick. She wrote plays, and one of them, *Percy*, was performed at Drury Lane.

When she was forty, Hannah abandoned her frequent visits to London and returned to Bristol. She discovered Ann Yearsley (q.v.), the Milkmaid poet and, with the help of friends, published a book of Ann's poetry.

Accompanied by her favourite sister, Martha, Hannah moved to a cottage at Wrington and dedicated herself to the poor and needy of Cheddar, a district later described by Charlotte Yonge in sombre terms:

> Wherever we turn, in almost every part of England we hear legends of the frightful neglect and inefficiency of the clergy at the end of the last century. Cheddar seems to have been unusually unfortunate: the incumbent absent, the curates serving three or four parishes at once, intoxication common among them as well as the farmers, and the moral degradation of the peasantry almost verging on savagery. (*Biographies of Good Women*, 1865)

The sisters became 'missionaries', hiring rooms, establishing schools, forming benefit clubs and distributing suitable books and tracts. They later bought a property near Wrington called Barley Wood and also built a house in Pulteney Street, Bath.

Hannah More outlived her sisters and, aged eighty-three, moved to Clifton, Bristol. She died there but was buried at Wrington.

LADY CELIA BRUNEL NOBLE

1870–1962
(née James)
Lived: 22 Royal
Crescent, Bath

Lady Celia Noble was a granddaughter of the brilliant engineer, Isambard Kingdom Brunel, who designed, among other things, the Clifton Suspension Bridge at Bristol. She lived for many years at 22 Royal Crescent, Bath, where she continued her life-long interest in music and the arts. Lady Celia was well-known as a society hostess. She also wrote *The Brunels: Father and Son*, (1938), of which she said: 'This book is no more than an attempt to set my great-grandfather and my grandfather upon their feet as living characters'. She died in Bath, aged ninety-two.

JULIANA POPJOY (OR PAPJOY)

1711?–1777
Popjoy's Restaurant,
Nash House, Saw Close,
Bath

Did you never hear tell of a Wiltshire belle
(No lady could well be fairer),
At Bishopstrow she was born, although
Not a woman there could bear her!
(W. Gurney Benham, *Beau Nash and Juliana Popjoy etc, c.* 1887)

Juliana Popjoy does not appear to have been at all concerned about

This was the splendid home of Beau Nash. The King of Bath, and his handsome and faithful mistress Juliana Popjoy. They spent the whole of the latter part of their lives here – until the Beau's death, in 1761, at the age of 86.

We preserve in this building all the high standards Beau Nash set for Bath. We think that Juliana Popjoy approves. Indeed, she is occasionally seen here, dressed in grey, and we suspect she has an eye on whether we are entertaining our guests as well as the Beau's entertained the Beau's friends in the same rooms.

the opinions of 'the folks of Bishopstrow'. She soon deserted Wiltshire and went to live in Bath, where she worked as a dressmaker and became the mistress of Beau Nash. (Beau Nash had arrived in Bath in 1705 and was soon appointed Master of the Ceremonies. For nearly forty years he ruled over the glittering social life there and was nicknamed 'The King of Bath'.)

Unfortunately almost everything written about Juliana has been based on contemporary gossip and many of the stories contradict each other. In her heyday she:

> Rode about the streets on a dapple-grey horse, carrying in her hand a many-thonged whip, which caused her to be known as 'Lady Betty Besom'. (Lewis Melville, *Bath under Beau Nash*, 1907)

She may have lived with Nash until his death in 1761 and then, poor and lonely, earned her living by gathering herbs and carrying messages. It seems almost unbelievable that she made her home in a tree, but when she died, in 1777, the *Gentleman's Magazine* printed this obituary:

> Juliana Papjoy, a singular character. For thirty or forty years she lived in a hollow tree, and never lay in a bed. She had been mistress to the famous Nash of Bath.

Whatever really happened, Juliana has never been entirely forgotten in Bath. When Beau Nash's last home (near the Theatre Royal), was converted into a restaurant some years ago, it was promptly named 'Popjoy's'.

JANE PORTER
1776–1850
ANNA MARIA PORTER
1780–1832
Plaque: Cloisters of Bristol Cathedral

Jane and Anna Maria Porter were both novelists and much admired in their day. Anna Maria's best known work, *The Hungarian Brothers* was published in 1807. Jane, possibly the more gifted of the two, wrote, among others: *The Scottish Chiefs* (1810) and, late in her life, *Sir Edward Seward's Narrative:*

The last work, published anonymously, while really a clever

fiction, had so much the appearance of genuine description that people everywhere hunted out their atlases to ascertain where the scene was situated. (J. Murch, *Mrs Barbauld and her Contemporaries*, 1877)

Both sisters lived for a while in Bristol and both of them died there. There is a memorial plaque to them in the cloisters of Bristol Cathedral.

SARAH SCOTT
1723–1795
(née Robinson)
Lived: Batheaston, near Bath

In 1762 a book was published called *A Description of Millenium Hall and the Country Adjacent, by a Gentleman on his Travels*. In fact, the author of the book was Mrs Sarah Scott. A sister of Elizabeth Montagu, the well-known society hostess and intellectual, Sarah married George Lewis Scott in 1751, but he treated her so atrociously that she was hurriedly removed by her family. Luckily, she had a close friend, Lady Bab (Barbara) Montagu, and, pooling their financial resources, they decided to live together in Bath. In 1754 they moved to Batheaston and there ran a school for twelve poor girls. This was the

inspiration for Sarah's *Millenium Hall*, the story of a group of women of independent means who establish a female Utopia:

There are twelve of us that live here. We have every one a house of two rooms, as you may see, beside other conveniences, and each a little garden; but though we are separate, we agree as well, perhaps better than if we lived together, and all help one another.

When Lady Bab died in 1765, Sarah was unable to carry on by herself. She still spent much of her time in Bath, but died at Catton, near Norwich, in Norfolk.

HARRIETTE ANNE SEYMOUR
1830–?
Born: Marksbury Rectory, Marksbury, near Bath

From her earliest years she had a great love of art, but it was not encouraged, as an elder sister was thought to have more genius, and their parents said 'One artist was enough in the family.' Her mind, which was very keen and subtle, developed in other ways, and the art instinct received little encouragement or help. (Ellen Clayton, *English Female Artists*, 1876)

Harriette's 'art instinct' revived, however, when what Ellen Clayton describes as her 'large share in the responsibilities of home life' came to an end. She immediately began her struggle to be taken seriously as an artist and, aged thirty-two, took private lessons at Clifton, Bristol, and also attended night classes there.
Harriette's attempts to study in Bristol, London and Brussels, were

continually interrupted by illness. Eventually she returned to the West Country, living on Dartmoor in the summer and at Porthleven, Cornwall, during the winter months. She continued to work in oils, water colour and crayon, and exhibited in London, Liverpool, Manchester, Plymouth and Falmouth. Much of her work concentrated on the local landscape, with titles such as *Sunset on the Cornish Coast, The Old Mill, Chagford* and *A Wild Night, Trebarwith Strand*.
Although we know that Harriette Seymour was still working when Ellen Clayton wrote about her in 1876, we have not been able to trace the date or place of her death.

ELLEN SHARPLES

1769–1849
(née Wallace)

ROLINDA SHARPLES

1793–1838
Buried: Upper Burial
Ground, Clifton Parish
Churchyard
Various works: Bristol
City Museum and Art
Gallery

Ellen and Rolinda Sharples were mother and daughter. They were also both artists and Rolinda left a delightful portrait of herself, working on a canvas, while her mother stands watching her with loving pride. The painting is owned by the Bristol City Museum and Art Gallery. The Sharples lived and worked in Bristol and are buried in the Upper Burial Ground of Clifton Parish Churchyard.

Ellen Wallace was living in Bath when she met James Sharples, a portrait painter. She was, it seems, attending his art classes when they fell in love and married. Their daughter, Rolinda, was born in 1793 and the family moved to America about three years later.

James Sharples became a successful portrait painter there and one of his best portraits was of George Washington. Ellen became an expert 'copier' of her husband's work and also began to specialize in needlework pictures of a very high standard, using fine black silk on a cream background. At an early age their daughter, Rolinda, also began to show signs of artistic talent. Ellen wrote:

> My dear Rolinda, now nine years of age, my inseparable companion, is always cheerful and in perfect good humour . . . of an active mind she is always employed, and as we are ready to instruct her, so far as we are competent, she advances in knowledge with great rapidity.

Mr Sharples died in New York in 1811 and Ellen promptly returned to England with her children Rolinda and James. Eventually they settled in Bristol, living at first in Clifton and later in St Vincent's Parade. Rolinda painted landscapes and portraits of local people, as well as records of Bristol life. She became an honorary member of the Society of British Artists and exhibited at the Royal Academy, London, in 1820. Her best-known works were *The Trial of Colonel Brererton* (1834) and *Clifton Racecourse* (1836?). She died of cancer aged only forty-five.

Ellen Sharples survived both her children:

> She died at the age of eighty . . . Having no heirs, it was most fitting that she decided as she did – on leaving her money and pictures to the above-named [Bristol Fine Arts Academy] – thus becoming the real foundress of Bristol's first art gallery. (Katharine McCook Knox, *The Sharples: Their Portraits of George Washington and his Contemporaries*, 1930)

Portrait of Ellen and Rolinda Sharples, painted by Rolinda Sharples

SARAH SIDDONS

1755–1831
(née Kemble)

Plaque: 33 The Paragon, Bath

Theatre Royal, Bath

The actress Sarah Siddons, born in Wales, once referred to herself as a 'child of Bath'. This was an acknowledgement of the period in her life when, after a temporary failure on the London stage, she retreated, in 1775, to the provinces, where she was a resounding success. James Boaden, in his *Memoirs of Mrs Siddons* (1827) remarked that:

> The charms of the Cotillion itself were resisted, and no nights at all in the Bath Theatre were attended by the fashionable world, but those on which Mrs Siddons acted.

In October 1782 she appeared once again in London. This time she was an instant and total success:

> Honours too and patronage came to her abundantly. The street before her lodgings in the Strand was crowded with the coaches of the nobility coming to call upon her. (Percy Fitzgerald, *Lives of the Kembles*, 1871)

Sarah Siddons died in London and was buried at St Mary's Church, Paddington Green. In Bath there is a plaque on 33 The Paragon, where she lived for several years. It was unveiled in 1922 by another great actress, Ellen Terry.

LILY SPENDER

1838–1895
(née Headland)
Lived and was
buried: Bath

In 1858 Lily Headland, aged twenty, married John Kent Spender, physician to the Mineral Water Hospital (later the Royal National Hospital) in Bath. She had eight children, lived in Bath for the rest of her life, and took an active interest in educational and social work there. She also wrote novels.

There are some women who seem to be able to produce romances, liberally spattered with purple prose, as easily and naturally as if they were breathing, and Lily Spender had this ability. Her novels, with titles such as *Her Own Fault* (1871), *Jocelyn's Mistake* (1875), and *A Strange Temptation* (1893), were immensely popular and very successful.

Here is a typically splendid sample of Lily Spender's writing style, from *The Wooing of Doris*, one of her last novels, published in 1895:

She gave a little shiver as she felt his fingers closing on hers. The sun was just dipping below the horizon, and swords dyed with blood were thrown out from its glowing disc, illuminating with their brilliant light the mists on the mountain sides, then fading and leaving them ghostly. She was conscious of a sudden chill as she hurried back to the hotel, her heart beating with such great thuds that it seemed to her as if others might hear it.

Lucky Doris!

ADA VACHELL

1866–1923
Plaque: Bristol Cathedral

Born in Wales, Ada moved to Bristol when she was nine years old. She remained there for the rest of her life, dedicating her energies to helping the underprivileged particularly the disabled. She started a Sunday class at her home, taught for a while at a training home for girls, helped to run a girls' club and, in 1895, when she was twenty-nine, founded the Guild of the Handicapped in

Bristol. Later she also initiated an Invalid Children's School there.

Ada Vachell actively sought out disabled people of all ages and persuaded them to join the Guild. Every year she took a group of the most seriously disabled away to the country for a fortnight and eventually opened a holiday home at Churchill, in Somerset. There is a plaque to her memory in Bristol Cathedral.

PAULE VÉZELAY (MARGERY WATSON-WILLIAMS)

1892–1984
Born: Clifton, Bristol

English Art bored me to tears . . . the English don't like originality in Art very much you know. (Television interview with Germaine Greer, 1984)

The artist Paule Vézelay was seen on television in July 1984, being interviewed by Germaine Greer for a series called 'Women of Our Century'. She had died a few months earlier at her home in Barnes, London.

Paule Vézelay was born Margery Watson-Williams in Clifton, Bristol. She attended the art school in Bristol when she was seventeen and moved on to the Slade, London, two years later. From the Slade she transferred to a small

school in Kensington, and studied there until war broke out in 1914.

During the war, she continued to work and, in 1918, exhibited at the New English Art Club. However, in 1926, she moved to Paris and changed her name to Paule Vézelay.

In Paris Paule felt at home – and free to work as she pleased. She exhibited regularly at the Salon des Surindépendents and began a lifelong friendship with the artists Jean Arp and his wife, Sophie. By the late 1930s she was beginning to be accepted as one of the leading abstract artists working in Paris at the time. Then came the Second World War.

Paule left France and returned to England, where she spent most of the war looking after her parents. To her disappointment she was not chosen as an official war artist, but was given permission to draw at the barrage balloon centre just outside Bristol.

When she returned to Paris in 1946 she found everything changed almost beyond recognition and, after a brief attempt to start again, she left for London. There, lonely and isolated, she eventually became interested in textile design and worked for Heal's. In 1949 she was made a member of the British Society of Industrial Artists and Designers.

After a period in the wilderness which lasted about ten years, Paule's work began to be exhibited once again. A show at the Grosvenor Galleries in London was later followed by one at Zabriskie's in New York and then, in 1983, the Tate: 'She was,' said Ronald Alley, keeper of the Modern Collection at the Tate, 'one of the first British artists to commit themselves totally and irrevocably to the Abstract movement.'

SUSANNA WINKWORTH
1820–1884

CATHERINE WINKWORTH
1827–1878
Plaque: Bristol Cathedral

Susanna and Catherine Winkworth were both born in London. They spent much of their early lives in Manchester but eventually settled in Clifton, Bristol. Susanna died and was buried at Clifton, and Catherine, although she was buried at Monnetier, near Geneva, Switzerland, has a large wall plaque to her memory in Bristol Cathedral.

Both sisters became German scholars. In 1853 Catherine's *Lyra Germanica* (translations of German hymns in common use) was published; in 1854 Susanna's *Theologia Germanica*.

Susanna was a philanthropist as well as a writer, and spent a great deal of time working for the poor and deprived in Bristol. Particularly interested in the problems of housing, she rented several houses in the poorest areas, had them repaired and let them out to tenants.

Catherine, deeply interested in encouraging higher education for women, became a governor of the Red Maid's School in Bristol, a promoter of Clifton High School for Girls, and a member of the Council of Cheltenham Ladies' College.

ANN YEARSLEY
1756–1806
Buried: Clifton Parish Churchyard, Clifton Hill, Bristol

On the axis of Love, wheels the Universe round,
In rotation continued, and thrifty;
While some tender minds at fifteen feel the wound,
And some hold it out till they're fifty.
(Ann Yearsley, untitled poem)

Ann Yearsley has become known as the Milkmaid poet – a title that is totally misleading. It gives the impression of gentle, placid country life and of a rosy-cheeked young woman composing poems in praise of Nature. Ann was not like that at all. She was, in fact, fiercely independent and often very angry.

Born in Bristol, where her mother sold milk from door to door, she received the minimum of education. She managed, however, to develop an interest in poetry, read what she could lay her hands on and then began to write. She married, started a family and took up selling milk herself. Then, one day, Ann was introduced to Hannah More (q.v.), writer and philanthropist, who lived in Bristol:

On my return from Sandleford, a copy of verses was shown to me, said to be written by a poor illiterate woman in this neighbourhood, who sells milk . . . When I went to see her, I observed a perfect simplicity in her

33

manners, without the least affectation or pretension of any kind: she neither attempted to raise my compassion by her distress, nor my admiration by her parts. (A prefatory letter by Hannah More to *Poems on Several Occasions*, 1787)

Hannah More decided to help Ann. She became her patron and had her poems published, realizing over six hundred pounds. Unfortunately, the deed of trust excluded any control by the author. Ann was furious and resentful, quarrelled bitterly with

Hannah and, when accused of ingratitude, hit back in verse:

> You, who thro' optics dim, so falsely view
> This wond'rous maze of things, and rend a part
> From the well-order'd whole, to fit your sense
> Low, groveling, and confin'd; say from what source
> Spring your all-wise opinions?
> (Ann Yearsley, *To Those who Accuse the Author of Ingratitude*

Unforgiving and unrepentent, Ann continued on her own. She wrote a five-act tragedy, *Earl Godwin* (1789), which was performed at both Bristol and Bath. The same year she hurled abuse at Levi Eames who, she said, had had her two sons horsewhipped for playing in one of his fields. (Mr Eames had just finished his term as Lord Mayor of Bristol):

> Hast thou read o'er the statutes of the land?
> In Magna-Charta hast thou ever found
> A *Mayor* trudging with his whip in hand,
> To give the school-boy many a *lawful* wound?
> (Ann Yearsley, *Stanzas of Woe* 1797)

Ann also started a Circulating Library at the Colonnade in Hot Wells, Bristol. She died at Melksham, but was buried in the churchyard of the old Clifton Parish Church.

Portrait of Ann Yearsley, the Milkmaid poet

CORNWALL

MABEL LUCIE ATTWELL

1879–1964
(Mrs Earnshaw)
Lived: 3 St Fimbarrus Terrace, Fowey

Fowey is a friendly, picturesque town with a charming and colourful harbour. It has a fascinating history which includes Place, the seat of the Treffry family, and several well-known residents and visitors. Less well-known is the fact that Mabel Lucie Attwell, artist, illustrator and writer, retired to Fowey, living at 3 St Fimbarrus Terrace, until her death in 1964.

Mabel Lucie Attwell was born in London and studied at the Regent Street Art School:

Finding herself bored by copying classical casts, she soon took to making spirited sketches 'out of her head' to illustrate her own fantasies and fairy stories. (*Times* obituary, 1964)

From these 'fantasies and fairy stories' sprang what can only be described as the Mabel Lucie Attwell cult. She illustrated editions of famous children's books, such as Charles Kingsley's *The Water Babies* and Lewis Carroll's *Alice in Wonderland*, and her famous chubby-children were used on textiles, toys, china and postcards. *Lucie Attwell's Annual* was published from 1922 to 1962, and many people still cherish Mabel Lucie Attwell memorabilia.

'BAL MAIDENS'

(Ceased their work
c. 1910)
Many mines throughout Cornwall, most notably the (now disused) Blue Hill Mines, St Agnes

Most of the work in connection with the dressing of tin and copper ores, which was too heavy for the children, was given to older women and girls known as 'Bal Maidens', great numbers of whom were always employed on the surface of Cornish mines. (A. K. Hamilton Jenkin, *The Cornish Miner*, 1927)

Bal Maidens did one of two different types of surface work in the mines. One job, known as 'spalling', meant standing out of doors and breaking up the larger rocks with long-handled hammers. The other, called 'bucking', consisted of breaking down the copper ore stones into small pieces on an anvil. To do this, the women sat, in cramped positions, in cold and draughty sheds.

In 1842 it was reported that, if a girl worked very hard indeed, she could earn the derisory sum of one shilling a day.

These Cornish Bal Maidens formed a close-knit social group:

shrewd, honest, respectable . . . sometimes rough in speech and generally plain-spoken enough in repartee, as anyone who addressed them disrespectfully soon found. (A. K. Hamilton Jenkin)

They also developed their own particular style of dress. A blouse, known as 'Garboldi' (Garibaldi) was tucked inside a long skirt and, over this, when walking to the mine, or back home at the end of the day, a white pinafore (replaced at work by a rough hessian apron). It was the head-dress that was unique. Sometimes known as a 'yard of cardboard', it was simply that – a piece of cardboard, worn across the head, with cotton print attached to it, falling down over the shoulders:

The spread of cheap education and the substitution of machinery for human labour has caused a complete disappearance of the Bal Maiden, although a few were employed at the Carn Brea Mines as recently as fourteen or fifteen years ago. Their disappearance has robbed the surface of a Cornish mine of one of its most picturesque and characteristic features. (A. K. Hamilton Jenkin)

MARY ANN BENETTO

1802–?

Tried: Truro

Among those brought before the Justices of Quarter Sessions at Truro in January 1827 was Mary Ann Benetto, a farmer's wife. Twenty-five years old and heavily pregnant, she was there on a charge of shop-lifting at St Austell.

Mary Ann had stolen a pair of braces and some pieces of printed cotton – articles of little value. Her husband was not poor and there appeared to be no logical reason for her behaviour. Unfortunately crime was said to be on the increase, and the Establishment set out to make examples. Mary Ann Benetto was savagely sentenced to transportation to a penal settlement for seven years.

One can only imagine the emotions that ran riot in the court on that day. Mary Ann's husband begged to be allowed to go in her place, but the Chairman of the Sessions, although 'much affected' when delivering the sentence, refused this desperate appeal.

So far it has not been established where the penal settlement was, whether Mary Ann was allowed to give birth before leaving, or when, if ever, she returned to Cornwall. Her punishment must have been considered particularly shocking as, over a hundred years later, Charles Henderson wrote:

> It was due to a Cornishman, Sir William Molesworth, as much as any other man, that the abominable practice of transportation was afterwards done away with. When poor Mary Ann was sentenced, her penalty was simple slavery of a brutal and disgusting kind. A generation earlier, she would have been hanged; a generation later, she would have been put in a female penitentiary; nowadays she would be looked after in a mental hospital. (*The West Briton and Cornwall Advertiser*, 16 January 1930)

And today . . . ?

TAMSON BLIGHT

fl. 1840

Lived: Helston

One night when Aunt Tammy Blight lay very ill, a farmer came in great trouble about his horse, which he said would surely die unless she could help. As she was too ill to be moved she called her little boy to her side and touched him, saying certain words. Then to the farmer she said, 'If you can *carry* my child to where the horse is, his touch shall cure it for I have passed my power on to him for this occasion.' He did as he was told, and the horse recovered. (*Old Cornwall*, Volume II, 1936)

There are many stories about Tamson Blight, the white witch of

Helston, and probably many more still to be discovered.

Tammy Blee, as she was known locally, was probably born in Redruth. She married a man whose name has been given as James Thomas, but she left him and set up on her own as a faith-healer and herbalist of exceptional ability. Many people believed implicitly in Tamson's powers:

> On one occasion a woman living near Helston had a child, which was affected with a mysterious sickness . . . As it was generally

believed in the neighbourhood that the child was 'ill-wished', the woman was advised to go to Helston in order to consult Tamson Blight. A visit was accordingly made, and the woman demanded of Tamson the name of her ill-wisher. This she refused to give but nevertheless . . . described the culprit in such detail that the woman 'immediately named the sorcerer' and returned home resolved to 'bring blood from her'. A few days later the supposedly guilty person passed the woman's door, upon which she rushed out and laid violent hands upon her, scratching her arm, till it bled. From that hour we are told the child began to mend. (A. K. Hamilton Jenkin, *Cornwall and the Cornish*, 1933)

It seems that Tamson Blight retained her remarkable powers to the end of her life:

Such was Tamson's fame that shortly before her death, when she was confined to her bed, people were . . . brought to her on stretchers, and laid beside her in her room, where from being entirely helpless, they were known to 'rise up and go down over stairs perfectly cured'. (A. K. Hamilton Jenkin)

THOMASINE BON-AVENTURE

c. 1440–1512
The College,
Week St Mary

Thomasine, a farmer's daughter born at Week St Mary, was noticed by a London merchant, who happened to ride past one day as she was tending her father's sheep.
Thomas Barnaby – or Richard Bunsby, depending on which version of the story one comes across – cast an admiring glance at Thomasine and promptly persuaded her to accompany him to London as a maidservant. Later, when his wife died, he married her and then died himself. Thomasine, now a wealthy young widow, soon married another merchant and later still married for a third time. Her last husband, John Percival, became Lord Mayor of London.
It is not known whether Dame Percival returned to visit Week St Mary. She certainly bequeathed valuable gifts to several churches in the area and also endowed a free Grammar School in Week itself. Part of this building, called The College, is still there.

ANGELA BRAZIL

1869–1947
The Warren, Polperro

I have just bought the cliffs and hillside between Polperro and Talland. I heard they were for sale, and I was so afraid a speculative builder might get them that I thought I had better save them before they could be spoilt. (Letter from Angela Brazil to Marie Stopes)

Polperro

The National Trust and, indeed, everyone who loves Cornwall, owes a debt of gratitude to Angela Brazil, that enthusiastic and prolific writer of girls'-school stories.
Born in Lancashire, Angela began writing her exceptionally popular books when she was thirty-six. She became a best-seller with titles such as *The Nicest Girl in the School* (1909), *The Jolliest Term on Record* (1915) and *Three Terms at Uplands* (1945).
After the First World War Angela Brazil bought a cottage in Polperro. It was her holiday home and she spent a great deal of time there. In 1922 she bought a piece of land nearby, known as Warren Field, for five hundred and fifty pounds. Later she added an adjoining strip and, when she died, she left it all to the National Trust.

It is known as The Warren, and described as 'a mile of cliff'.

In her book *A Fortunate Term* (1921), Angela Brazil introduced Polperro – under the assumed name of Chagford:

Though it was only the first of February, the village, owing to the large number of its half-exotic shrubs, was framed in a setting of green, among which the little colour-washed houses shone like flowers.

GRACEY BRINEY (OR HICHENS)

1778–1869
Lived: Redruth

1869: Gracey Briney, whose real name was Grace Hichens died at Redruth. Age 91. A few weeks before she died she went to St Dominick 50 miles from Redruth for a load of cherries . . . For 35 years before her death she wore the same style clothes – a blue cloth tailcoat with brass buttons, a high hat, petticoats, stockings and shoes. (*Annals of an ancient Cornish Town – Redruth*)

The death of Gracey Briney caused considerable local interest, not only because she wore eccentric clothes but because she was probably the only woman in Cornwall to have done a man's work in the mines.

A strong and active young woman, Gracey worked in the mines and was offered the difficult and dangerous job of 'kibble lander'. This involved landing the kibble (full container) as it reached the surface, by seizing it with an iron pot-crook and pulling it off the mouth of the shaft onto the landing stage.

No one will ever know what trials she had to endure before her acceptance in a man's world, but accepted she was, and became a frequent visitor at the Pick and Gad public house, where she smoked a pipe and drank beer with the best.

As she grew older she became quite a celebrity, and clearly enjoyed her reputation. *The Cornish Magazine and Devon Miscellany* of 1885 described Gracey in old age:

Her hair flowed carelessly down her back; and she had a grey moustache. After ceasing to work at the mine . . . she sold fish, driving a horse and cart with the whip tied across her shoulder when not in use. She was a constant attendant at the Redruth weekly market and was most industrious.

MARIA BRONTË

1783–1821
(née Branwell)

ELIZABETH BRANWELL

1776–1842
Born: St Michael's Mount

The Branwells were a large family – Maria and Elizabeth being two of eleven children. Most of them grew up in a house that overlooked Mount's Bay, St Michael's Mount, but they later moved to 25 Chapel Street, Penzance.

In 1812 when she was twenty-nine years old, Maria left Cornwall to visit an uncle in Yorkshire. She met the Reverend Patrick Brontë there, married him, and never returned home. Within eight years she had given birth to six children, two of whom died young. Of the other four, Branwell, the son, was the 'black sheep' but her three daughters, Charlotte, Emily and Anne, all became novelists.

Maria Brontë died in 1821, aged only thirty-eight, but her sister Elizabeth soon arrived from Cornwall to look after the children. She missed her friends, missed the flowers and trees of the West Country, 'and particularly dreaded the cold arising from the floors in the passages and parlours of Haworth Parsonage'. However, she made the best of it and certainly must have enlivened the atmosphere with her own brand of gaiety, humour – and appearance. A friend of Charlotte's, Ellen Nussey, described her:

She wore caps large enough for half-a-dozen of the present fashion, and a front of light auburn curls over her forehead . . . She talked a great deal about her younger days; the gaieties of her dear native Penzance, in Cornwall. (Daphne Du Maurier, *Vanishing Cornwall*, 1967)

DOROTHY MARY ROWENA CADE

1894–1983

Founded: Minack Theatre, Porthcurno

The theatre, now happily established in perpetuity as a Trust, will continue and be her lasting memorial but it is not only for this, her life-work, that she will be remembered. She was a character who adorned almost everything she touched. Her talents lay especially in her creative hands but it was her compulsive personality, her old-fashioned charm and her sometimes ruthless single-mindedness of purpose which impressed those who encountered her. (*Times* obituary, 1983)

39

In 1932, Rowena Cade founded the Minack Theatre at Porthcurno near Land's End. A production of *The Tempest*, in the natural amphitheatre that lay in the grounds of her own home, inspired her to build a permanent open-air theatre there. With the help of her gardener, Billy Rawlings, she designed and constructed the Minack, poised on the edge of the cliffs with its stunning backdrop of sea, sky and wheeling birds.

The rest of her life was spent organizing annual seasons of plays sometimes directing productions herself, and always working on improvements to the building. Over the years she carved the names and dates of past productions onto the backs of the seats, and in 1982 she attended a jubilee production of *The Tempest* in the theatre she had created fifty years earlier.

THE CALEDONIA SHIP'S FIGUREHEAD

1842
St Morwenna's
Churchyard,
Morwenstow

In September 1842, the *Caledonia* was wrecked off the coast of northern Cornwall.

The Reverend Robert Hawker, vicar of St Morwenna's Church, Morwenstow, was roused by a member of the household who knocked on his bedroom door shouting 'Oh, sir, there are dead men on Vicarage Rocks!'

The tragic task of dragging the bodies of drowned sailors on to dry land, and then carrying them up the steep path to the vicarage, was carried out by the vicar and some of his parishioners. Of a crew of ten, only one survived. The rest were buried in St Morwenna's churchyard, and the Reverend Hawker had the ship's figurehead placed over the grave of the captain.

Painted a ghostly white, and staring remotely into the distance, Caledonia is a strange little figure. She bears a sword and shield, and her pointed feet, raised above the grass, give the impression that she is longing to dance off towards the sea.

JOAN CARTHEW

Date unknown
Epitaph: St Ewe
Churchyard (epitaph no
longer exists)

The following epitaph is said to have been found on a tombstone in the churchyard of St Ewe. Not surprisingly, it has been quoted in several anthologies on Cornwall. For those who may have missed it, it is well worth quoting again:

Here lies the body of Joan Carthew
Born at St Mewan, died at St Ewe;
Children had she five,
Three is dead and two's alive:
They that are dead choosin' rather
To die with mother than live with father.

MARY ANN DAVENPORT

1759–1843
(née Harvey)
Born: Launceston

It was said of Mrs Jordan that her laugh would have made the fortune of any actress . . . But Mrs Davenport's strong point was her scream . . . She was of primary utility in a theatre as the representative of low, vulgar and antiquated characters. (*Authentic Memoirs of the Green Room*, 1806)

Mary Ann Davenport was an excellent character-actress. Born in Launceston, Cornwall, she was 'educated at Bath and made her first appearance on stage there as Lappet, in a play entitled *The Miser*. She spent two seasons in Bath before moving to Exeter, where she married Mr Davenport, a fellow actor.

Mary Ann's style and talent was considerable. In 1794 she made her first appearance in London at Covent Garden as Mrs Hardcastle in Oliver Goldsmith's *She Stoops to Conquer*. She was seldom out of work.

At the age of eighty-four Mary Ann Davenport was run over by a dray. She died in St Bartholomew's Hospital.

The *Caledonia* ship's figurehead in St Morwenna's Churchyard

MARY, LADY DRAKE

d. 1583
(née Newman)
Mary Newman's Cottage,
Saltash

Mary was the first wife of Sir
Francis Drake, that glamorous,
seafaring, swashbuckling
Elizabethan credited with the
defeat of the Spanish Armada. She
was born at Saltash, in Cornwall,
and in 1569 married Drake in the
church at St Budeaux, just across
the Tamar, in Devon.

As his wife she became Lady
Mayoress of Plymouth. She died in
1583 and was buried in the church
where she had been married, with
nothing to mark her grave. As
Arthur Mee in *The King's
England: Devon* (1938) remarked,
she was 'One of the least known
wives in the history of our famous
men.' Her name has, surprisingly,
survived.

The little cottage in Culver
Road, Saltash, where she is said to
have been born, has been repaired
and restored by the Tamar
Protection Society. This dedicated
group laboured for several years,
finding, among other treasures, a
complete Tudor fireplace behind
some rough pine panelling. Mary
Newman's Cottage was opened in
1984 and won the Cornish
Buildings Group Award. When we
visited Saltash in 1985, the cottage
was open twice a week, but the
Tamar Protection Society hope to
be able to open it more often in the
future.

Mary Newman's cottage

CHARLOTTE DYMOND

1826–1844

Monument: Roughtor, Bodmin Moor

From Camelford, follow the Roughtor road as far as it leads and you will find yourself in the National Trust car park on the edge of Bodmin Moor. From the car park, cross the bridge over the stream and then turn sharp right. A

little further on, isolated and incongruous, stands a simple stone monument. The inscription, now very difficult to decipher, reads:

Monument erected by public subscription in memory of Charlotte Dymond who was murdered by Matthew Weeks, Sunday April 14th, 1844.

Both Charlotte and Matthew lived and worked at Penhale Farm, owned by a Mrs Peters, on Bodmin Moor. Charlotte was a milkmaid, Matthew a general farm-worker, said to have been slightly crippled, and they began walking out together. One particular Sunday they went off across the moors. Neither of them returned.

Charlotte's body was found some time later near Roughtor Ford – her throat had been cut.

Matthew was caught at the Hoe, Plymouth. He was tried, and freely admitted his responsibility. Whether it was provoked by real or imagined jealousy will never be known but, during his evidence, he described with vivid simplicity the circumstances:

I told her I had seen her in a 'situation' with some young men that was disgraceful to her. She then said 'I shall do as I like. I shall have nothing more to do with you.' I took out my knife and then replaced it. But on her repeating the phrase I made a cut at her throat from behind. She immediately fell backwards, the blood gushing out in a large stream and exclaimed while falling, 'Lord have mercy on me.'

Matthew Weeks was executed at Bodmin Gaol. Thousands came to see him die.

Charlotte Dymond was buried in Davidstow Churchyard. Her ghost is said to haunt the place where she was murdered.

ST ENDELIENTA

Sixth century
Collegiate Church of St Endelienta, St Endellion

Among the many women saints in Cornwall, St Endelienta is perhaps the gentlest – and yet she is the one whose presence seems to linger most persistently in her church at St Endellion, high above Port Isaac on the north coast.

According to legend, St Endelienta was one of the daughters of a Welsh king. With some of her sisters she came to Cornwall to preach the gospel, and became a hermit. Owning nothing but a cow, she lived entirely off its milk.

One day her cow strayed onto land belonging to the Lord of Trentinney. He promptly killed the trespassing animal. Endelienta's godfather – said to have been King Arthur – equally promptly slew the Lord of Trentinney, but Endelienta forgave her enemy, and miraculously brought him back to life.

Before she herself died she asked that her body should be placed on a cart drawn by year-old cattle, and that she should be buried wherever they first stopped to rest. Her wishes were carried out and she was buried on the spot where the Collegiate Church of St Endelienta now stands.

For more than twenty years there has been a Festival of Music and Drama at St Endellion. Especially commissioned for the Festival, Diana Burrell's *Missa Sancte Endeliente* was first performed there in 1980. It is based on the traditional Latin Mass, sections of the liturgy in Cornish, and a hymn to St Endelienta, written by Nicholas Roscarrock in 1633:

> Strive we to imitate thy virtues rare,
> Thy faith, hope, charity, thy humble mind,
> Thy chasteness, meekness, and thy diet spare,
> And, that which in this world is hard to find,
> The love which thou to enemy didst show,
> Reviving him who sought thy overthrow.

CELIA FIENNES

1662–1741
Born: Wiltshire; travelled across Cornwall

Celia Fiennes, the famous traveller, arrived in Cornwall in 1698. She rode to Land's End on horseback and although the journey was both exhausting and difficult ('In the further west, the miles are very long ones') she found it well worth the effort:

> Thence I went over the heath to St Austell, which is a little market town where I lay . . . Here was a pretty good dining room and chamber within it, and very neat country women. My landlady brought me one of the West-country tarts; this was the first I met with, though I had asked for them in many places in Somerset and Devonshire. It is an apple pie with a custard all on the top. . . They scald their cream and milk in most parts of these countries, and so it is a sort of clouted cream as we call it, with a little sugar, and so put on top of the apple pie. (Celia Fiennes, *Through England on a Side-saddle*)

Celia died in London but was buried at Newton Toney, in Wiltshire.

ELIZABETH ADELA FORBES STANHOPE

1859–1912
(née Armstrong)
Married: St Peter's Church, Newlyn

Correct draughtsmanship, always her strong point, came to be a cult with her . . . and the masterly building of the framework underlying her vigorous colour became more and more a feature. (Mrs Lionel Birch, *Stanhope A. Forbes, A. R. A. and Elizabeth Stanhope Forbes*, 1906)

Elizabeth Armstrong was born in Canada. As a young girl she travelled to England with her mother, and studied at the South Kensington Art Schools. Her father died while they were away and mother and daughter decided to stay in Europe. When Elizabeth had completed her studies they moved to Brittany (France).

> While at Pont-Aven, I continually heard rumours of a certain young Englishman, working in the adjacent

town of Quimperlé, with whom in years to come I was destined to make acquaintance.

In 1885 Elizabeth and her mother arrived in the flourishing art colony at Newlyn, Cornwall, and it was there that Elizabeth finally met the 'certain young Englishman', Stanhope Alexander Forbes. They were married in the little church of St Peter, in 1889. Elizabeth gave birth to a son and, in 1899, she and her husband founded a busy and successful art school in Newlyn.

ANNA MARIA FOX

1815–1897
Royal Cornwall
Polytechnic Society,
Church Street, Falmouth

Anna Maria and Caroline Fox (q.v.) were sisters, Quakers, and the daughters of Robert Fox, shipping agent and noted amateur scientist. They were both born at Falmouth and, with their brother Barclay, received a stimulating education that included mathematics, history, geography, poetry and languages. They were also encouraged to swim, play cricket and practise archery. This lively upbringing, combined with their Quaker background, produced two exceptionally talented and interesting women.

Anna Maria, the elder, conceived the idea for the Royal Cornwall Polytechnic Society in Falmouth. Established and supported financially by the Foxes, the Polytechnic was founded in 1833, its aim to promote education, art, science, commerce and manufacture. It was the first of its kind to be set up in the provinces.

Both sisters actively supported the Society and Anna Maria, the artist of the family, frequently exhibited there.

She did much to promote the arts and continued painting well into old age. It was to her memory that the Art School at Falmouth was dedicated in 1902.

CAROLINE FOX

1819–1871
Buried: Budock Quaker
Burial Ground

Jan. 21 1849 – Driving to Falmouth, a pig attached itself to the cortège and made us even more remarkable than usual. Piggy and Dory (the dog) scampering on side by side, and playing like frolicsome children, spite of all we could do to turn the incipient Bacon back to his former path in life. (Caroline Fox, *Memories of Old Friends*, 1882)

Caroline, the younger of the Fox sisters, kept a diary throughout her life. A selection from this diary was published in 1882, after her death, under the title *Memories of Old Friends, Being Extracts from the Journals and Letters of Caroline Fox of Penjerrick, Cornwall, from 1835 to 1871.*

The fascination of Caroline's journal has mainly been due to her descriptions of the many famous and interesting people she met during her lifetime, ranging from John Stuart Mill, Thomas Carlyle and Alfred Tennyson, to the journalist, John Sterling and Holman Hunt, the artist.

She spent much of her life caring for the old, ill and under-privileged but her own health gradually deteriorated and she died aged only fifty-two.

Both the Fox sisters were buried in the Budock Quaker Burial Ground.

ANN GLANVILLE

1796–1880
(née Warring)
Born and lived: Saltash

Ann was born at Saltash. She came from a waterman's family and married into one, helping her husband to ferry passengers and goods over to Devonport:

Sometimes she rowed out officers to their ships, sometimes conveyed play-actors over from Plymouth into Cornwall, and on the great event of the elections at Saltash, candidates, electors, pot-boilers, political orators. Meat and vegetables went over in these boats to Plymouth market: a gentleman remembers Ann bringing round as many as seventy or eighty bags of corn in her boat from South Pool, pulling the great cargo alone, conveying it from Sutton Pool to Butt's Head Mill, a point two miles above Saltash. (Sabine Baring-Gould, *Cornish Characters and Strange Events*, 1909)

Ann Glanville had fourteen children and when her husband fell ill, she supported the whole family by herself.

As light relief this amazing woman rowed in regattas as stroke in the Saltash Women's crew, competing at Hull, Liverpool and Portsmouth. They seldom lost a race and, on one never-to-be-forgotten occasion in 1850, they rowed at Le Havre against a (male) French crew. It was during this race that Ann was heard to yell 'Bend your backs to it, maidens – and hoorah for old England!' They won – by one hundred yards.

EMMA LAVINIA HARDY

1840–1912 (née Gifford)
Memorial: St Julitta Church, St Juliot

I found her out there
On a slope few see,
That falls westwardly
To the salt-edged air,
Where the ocean breaks
On the purple strand,
And the hurricane shakes
The solid land.
(Thomas Hardy)

Emma Gifford was born and brought up in Plymouth, Devon, but in 1860 the family moved to Cornwall. There, her sister Helen married the Vicar of St Julitta Church, St Juliot, and Emma went to live with them at the Rectory:

I enjoyed the place immensely, and helped my sister in the house affairs, visiting the parish folk and playing the harmonium on Sundays. The splendid air made me strong and healthy, with red cheeks. (Emma Hardy, *Some Recollections*, 1979)

The church at St Juliot was in a bad state of repair and in 1870, a young architect's assistant, Thomas Hardy, was sent to inspect the old building and make a report. He arrived at the Rectory one Monday evening in March and it was Emma who opened the door. 'I was immediately arrested by his familiar appearance,' she wrote later, 'as if I had seen him in a dream.'

The attraction was mutual and, for the next few years, Thomas Hardy visited Emma regularly. In 1874, the year that his novel *Far From the Madding Crowd* was

published, they were married in London.

Their marriage was not an outstanding success, although neither – as some Hardy biographers suggest – was it a total failure. Emma was the inspiration for *A Pair of Blue Eyes*, and she encouraged and helped her husband enormously with his writing. The breakdown came much later, particularly after the publication of *Jude the Obscure* (1895), which, casting doubt on the Established Church and the sanctity of marriage, is said to have upset Emma deeply. She also found their relationship much more difficult after Hardy's rapid rise to fame.

Towards the end they were barely speaking to each other, and Emma poured all her bitterness into her diary. When she died in 1912 she was buried in Stinsford Churchyard, Dorset, and very soon after this Thomas Hardy made a pilgrimage to the places that she loved most in Devon and Cornwall. He arranged for a memorial to her in the church at St Juliot, and wrote some beautiful and very moving poems about her as a young woman, when they had first met in Cornwall.

ELIZABETH HEARD

1788–1867
Memorial: Truro Cathedral

By 1854 *The West Briton and Cornwall Advertiser* had become the most widely read newspaper in Cornwall, easily outstripping its nearest rival, the *Royal Cornwall Gazette*. It was printed and published by a woman, Elizabeth Heard.

Elizabeth's husband, John Heard, the original publisher, had died in 1823, at the age of forty-two. Three weeks after his death, Elizabeth's name appeared for the first time in the imprint of *The West Briton* – and remained there for the next forty-four years. She became well known, not only as a highly efficient businesswoman but also as someone approachable and sympathetic. Many Cornish writers, both established and aspiring, came to her parlour above the stationer's and bookseller's shop in Boscawen Street, Truro, to discuss their hopes, fears and futures over a dish of tea.

Elizabeth's second son, Edward Goodridge Heard, trained and influenced by his mother, took over *The West Briton* after her death in 1867.

There is a memorial window to Elizabeth Heard in Truro Cathedral.

BARBARA HEPWORTH

1903–1975
Barbara Hepworth Museum, Trewyn Studio, St Ives

Finding Trewyn Studio was a sort of magic. For ten years I had passed by with my shopping bags not knowing what lay behind the twenty foot walls . . . Here was a studio, a yard and garden where I could work in open air and space. A friend accompanied me to the auction to bid for me and asked me what my bid was. I said 'I will stop you when it is beyond my figure.' The first bid was far beyond my figure and, according to my friends, I went pale green and fainted – so the bidding went on and I got the place.

Barbara Hepworth, born in Yorkshire and trained at Leeds, London and in Italy, became one

47

of the greatest abstract sculptors of this century.

In 1939, with her second husband, the painter Ben Nicholson, she moved with her family to Cornwall, and St Ives became her home for the rest of her life.

In 1949 she discovered and bought Trewyn Studio and, twenty-six years later, she died tragically in a fire there. In October 1980 – according to Barbara Hepworth's own wishes – the artist's daughters and the executors of her estate, gave the studio and its contents to the nation. The Trustees of the Tate Gallery are responsible for its care and maintenance . . . Finding Trewyn Studio is still 'a sort of magic'.

In the gardens of Trewyn Studio, St Ives

ST IA
Martyred c. 450
St Ia's Church, St Ives

Once upon a time there was a girl called Ia, who lived in Ireland. One day she stepped on to a leaf, and floated gently across the sea to Cornwall.

That is the legend. Much more prosaic – but probably nearer the truth – is the story that a young Irishwoman, called Ia, accompanied by her brother Ercus and a few friends, arrived in Cornwall some time in the middle of the fifth century. They were missionaries.

Unfortunately the Cornish were

48

in no mood to be converted, and fairly soon the dedicated little band had been martyred near the mouth of the Hayle River.

It seems that before her death, Ia had built herself a cell near the sea and, gradually, a small village began to develop on the site. This eventually became the town of St Ives, with a church named St Ia's.

FRYNIWYD TENNYSON JESSE

1888–1958
(Mrs Harwood)
Lived: Myrtle Cottage, Newlyn

I started life as an art student and have found even my slight knowledge of drawing and painting invaluable to me in writing, as it does enable one to see. I am very fond of flying, and my chief passion is murder.
(F. Tennyson Jesse)

This tongue-in-cheek statement refers to Fryniwyd Tennyson Jesse's fascination with the background and psychology of murder. A brilliant criminologist, she edited six volumes of the *Notable British Trials* series and her own *Murder and its Motives* was published in 1924. She also wrote a novel, *A Pin to See the Peep-Show* (1934), based on the Thompson-Bywaters case in 1922, where a young woman's lover murders her husband and they are both executed for the crime.

F. Tennyson Jesse's strong link with Cornwall came through her mother, who was descended from a long line of Cornish seafarers. Although Fryniwyd was born in Kent, she studied art at the Stanhope Forbes (q.v.) School at Newlyn.

Later she became one of the very few women journalists to report from the front in the 1914–18 war. In 1918 she married the playwright H. M. Harwood, and collaborated with him on a number of plays, including *Billeted* (1917) and *How to be Healthy Though Married* (1930).

Several of her novels, *A Pin to See the Peep-Show*, *The Lacquer Lady* (1929) and *Moonraker* (1927) have recently been republished by Virago. *Moonraker*, a short but vivid adventure story, begins, and ends, in Cornwall.

MARY JEWELS

1902–1978
(née Tregurtha)
Lived: Vine Cottage, Newlyn

I have been influenced by nobody and entirely self-taught. A true Celt loving my Cornwall, its lovely stone hedges and the beautiful blue sea with puff-ball clouds and little fishing coves and corn in stooks – what could one wish for more? (Mary Jewels, quoted in *Britain's Art Colony by the Sea*, Denys Val Baker, 1959)

Mary Jewels was born in Newlyn, Cornwall. Her family had lived in Vine Cottage since 1812 and she was interviewed there in 1977, the year before she died, as one of 'the last of the local people who can recall clearly, and who were involved with the celebrated "Newlyn School"' (Frank Ruhrmund, *Cornish Life*, 1977).

Although she was very involved with the Newlyn group, Mary had no formal art training. It seems that one day, when she was about eighteen, the artist, Cedric Morris, gave her a canvas and paint and suggested that she should try to cover the canvas by the evening. Mary painted for the rest of her life. She was encouraged by Augustus John, who praised her work in an article he wrote for *Vogue*:

> She shows landscapes that are remarkable in the intensity of their earth-feeling. They blaze in the sight and are almost menacing in their hint of place-magic.

Mary Jewels became known as a naive artist, (the phrase primitive annoyed her), and most of her work was based on her deep understanding of Cornwall.

MARY KELYNACK

1766–1855
(née Tresize)
Lived: Dock Lane,
Penzance

Mary Kelynack was born near Madron and became a jowster, or fish-seller, like her well-known predecessor, Dolly Pentreath (q.v.). Most of her life was spent working hard and earning very little but, in October 1851, the year of the Great Exhibition in London, she suddenly became news. Although they misspelt her name, *The Illustrated London News* told her story:

> LONGEVITY AT THE GREAT EXHIBITION
> Amongst the many remarkable circumstances in connexion with the Great Exhibition, is the extraordinary number of persons of great ages who have journeyed long distances to see the World's Fair . . . On Tuesday, among the visitors at the Mansion-House was Mary Callinack, eighty-four years of age, who had travelled on foot from Penzance, carrying a basket on her head, with the object of visiting the Exhibition, and of paying her respects personally to the Lord Mayor and Lady Mayoress. As soon as the ordinary business was finished,

the aged woman entered the Justice room when the Lord Mayor, addressing her, said 'Well, I understand, Mrs Callinack, you have come to see me?' She replied, 'Yes, God bless you; I never was in such a place as this; I have come up asking for a small sum of money – I am 84.'

According to the *Illustrated London News*, the Lord Mayor then gave Mary a sovereign – at which she burst into tears and said 'Now I shall be able to get back.' The article continued:

> She was born in the parish of Paul, near Penzance, on Christmas-Day, 1766, so that she has nearly completed her 85th year. To visit the present Exhibition she walked the entire distance from Penzance, nearly 300 miles . . . She possesses her faculties unimpaired; is very cheerful; has a considerable amount of humour in her composition; and is withal a woman of strong common sense . . . She is fully aware that she has made herself somewhat famous.

Mary Kelynack died in Penzance three years later and was buried in St Mary's Churchyard there.

DAME MARY KILLIGREW

***fl.* 1582**
(née Wolverston)
Buried: St Budock's
Church, Falmouth

The Killigrews were a famous Cornish family who had virtually founded Falmouth and built Arwenack Manor there. They were powerful and wealthy but an incident in the late sixteenth century proved that their lives were not necessarily respectable. Over the years the story of Dame Mary Killigrew's act of piracy has become altered almost beyond recognition, but a close scrutiny reveals facts as fascinating as fiction.

In January 1582, loaded with cargo and seeking shelter from the winter gales, a Spanish ship, the *Lady of St Sebastian*, arrived at Falmouth and cast anchor. The owners, John de Chavis and Philip

May 5 1582. Examinations taken at Penryn before Sir Ric. Greynville and Mr Edmond Tremayne touching the taking away of the Spanish ship out of the harbour of Falmouth.

de Oryo, went ashore and took rooms at Penryn.

On 7 January, in the evening, the ship was boarded by a group of men, who bound the Spanish sailors, took over the ship and set sail. A few sailors, who had resisted, were thrown overboard.

The Killigrew servants were immediately suspected, but a local inn-keeper, Elizabeth Bowden, solemnly swore that they had all been at her inn that night. An open verdict was returned at the preliminary hearing.

However, de Chavis and de Oryo persevered and laid their complaint before higher authorities. An investigation began at Penryn in May. Two of Dame Mary's servants admitted that she had instructed them, with others, to board the Spanish ship. When they had taken it, they had returned to their boat, 'with sundry bolts of Hollands and leather', and swiftly returned to shore, where they moored by the smith's forge. Meanwhile their accomplices were heading the Spanish ship towards Ireland.

The plunder was taken to Arwenack Manor and was divided between their mistress, one of her relations and various maidservants. However, Dame Mary was said to have been so irritated that the spoils were not as valuable as she had hoped that she kept most of it herself. The servants were sworn to secrecy and the leather was buried in the garden.

Punishment was inevitable and some paid with their lives, but Dame Mary Killigrew, although she was tried for piracy, was pardoned. Later she was buried with her husband in St Budock's, the ancient parish church of Falmouth.

The Killigrew Monument in St Budock's Church, Falmouth

DAME LAURA KNIGHT

1877–1970
(née Johnson)
Lived: Newlyn and Lamorna

Cornwall is not like any other sort of country – it's no use trying to compare it with any other place. There are times when you think everything is quite ordinary; and there are times when you feel you are not properly you, but someone else whom you don't in the least know; and an atmosphere prevails which takes away any sense or belief you have ever had, and you don't know why, but you aren't in England any more. (Laura Knight, *The Magic of a Line*, 1965)

Laura Johnson was born in Nottingham and trained at Nottingham School of Art. She married Harold Knight, also an artist, in 1903 and in 1910 she and

her husband arrived in Cornwall. They lived and worked at Newlyn and Lamorna, where Laura painted *Daughters of the Sun*, causing a local scandal by using London models who were not in the least self-conscious about posing in the nude.

The Knights stayed in Cornwall for eight years before moving to London. Laura became very well known for her paintings of dancers, the theatre and circus life. During the Second World War she was appointed an official war artist, finally working at the Nuremberg Trials in 1946.

MERMAID (OF ZENNOR)

Zennor Church, Zennor

If you are not fortunate enough to catch a glimpse of a mermaid in her natural habitat in Cornwall, you can, at least, study some of their portraits in various churches.

The most famous of these is the mermaid carved on a bench-end in the church at Zennor.

She is the mermaid who bewitched Matthew Trewhella, a young man of the village. Matthew sang in the church choir and, one Sunday, so the legend goes, a beautiful woman in a long dress appeared and stood at the back of the church. She stared at Matthew throughout the service, but vanished just before it was over. Exactly the same thing happened on the second Sunday but, on her third appearance, Matthew followed her out of the church and down the stream that led to Pendour Cove. He was never seen again.

In 1963 an opera called *Morvoren*, by Philip Cannon, was first performed. It was based on the haunting story of the mermaid of Zennor:

> It is said that if you listen carefully on a warm summer's night you can hear the pair of lovers singing together.

The mermaid of Zennor

THE MERRY MAIDENS (STONE CIRCLE)

Near Land's End

In the wild and beautiful countryside west of Penzance there are many reminders of the people who occupied the area long before 'history' began. Among these remains are stone circles of the kind that are scattered all over Britain. All of them have magic, legend and fantasy woven around their existence and, in Cornwall, many of these stories concern young women.

Not far from Land's End, for instance, in the middle of a field, stands the circle of nineteen stones known as the Merry Maidens. Long ago, so the story goes, nineteen local girls dared each other to dance there one Sunday night. They were found the next morning – turned to stone.

It is said that anyone brave enough to visit the field at night during the full moon might see the girls dancing again in their proper forms.

Who knows, however, what price one might have to pay for such foolish curiosity!

Posing with the Merry Maidens

DAME FANNY MOODY

1866–1945
Born: Redruth

Fanny Moody, who became known as the Cornish nightingale, and who sang Tatyana in the first English performance of Tchaikovsky's *Eugene Onegin*, was born in Redruth. She showed musical talent from an early age, giving recitals and singing at local concerts. Educated at the Girls' High School in Redruth, she left Cornwall at the age of eighteen and studied singing in London. Her professional début was at Liverpool, where she sang Arline in *The Bohemian Girl*, as a member of the Carl Rosa Opera Company:

> her pleasant light soprano voice combined with her talent as an actress and her personal charm soon established her reputation. (*Times* obituary, 1945)

In 1890 Fanny sang at Drury Lane in London, and also married Charles Southcote Mansergh, a fellow-singer. Later they established their own company, the Moody-Manners Opera, and travelled to South Africa, where they sang at the Theatre Royal in Johannesburg. The Cornish miners there presented Fanny with a diamond tiara, which included the Cornish arms and motto, 'One and All'.

Much later, in 1940, a letter from Fanny Moody Manners appeared in *The West Briton*. It began:

> To my dear Cornish people,
> I have today sent the lovely diamond tiara, which the Cornish miners gave me in Johannesburg, to the British Red Cross. It will be sold to help the maimed and wounded of those who are so bravely defending us in this awful war; and I am sure that every one of you will approve of my action.

53

ST MORWENNA

Fifth century

Morwenstow Church,
Morwenstow

There are several versions of the life of St Morwenna – and as many alternative theories as to why the church at Morwenstow was named after her.

Legend assures us that she was the daughter of a Welsh king, Brychan, and that she was so unusually good and wise that she was invited to the Saxon court of King Ethelwolf, to teach his daughters. She remained there for many years and, when the king asked her what she would like as a reward for all her work, Morwenna requested a specific area in Cornwall where she could found a church: it was the wild and beautiful place now known as Morwenstow.

It is said that she carried a stone up from the beach on her head, and that where she first laid it down to rest water gushed out of the ground. This spring later became known as St Morwenna's Well. The second place that she chose to put the stone down was the site for her church.

When she was very ill her brother, St Nectan, came over from Hartland to nurse her and, as she was dying, she asked him to raise her up so that she could see the distant mountains of Wales.

The saint herself is thought to be the figure in the seven-hundred-year-old wall painting in the chancel, and she also appears in a painted window on the east side of the church.

DOROTHY ('DOLLY') PENTREATH

c. 1692–1777
(née Jeffery)

Memorial: Paul Parish
Church, Mousehole

When Dolly Pentreath died, an epitaph was written for her in Cornish. Translated, it read:

Old Dolly Pentreath, aged a hundred and two
Died and buried in Paul Parish too,
Not in the Church with people high
But in the churchyard doth old Dolly lie.

Sadly this epitaph was never used, perhaps because the author had been over-enthusiastic about Dolly's age – she was certainly not 'a hundred and two', but about eighty-five.

Dorothy Pentreath was one of a hardy breed called 'jowsters' – fish-sellers. These women carried their load round the countryside, walking for miles with heavy baskets slung on their backs. She lived in the village of Mousehole, and there is a plaque on a tiny cottage near the harbour:

Here lived Dolly Pentreath, one of the last speakers of the Cornish language as her native tongue. Died Dec. 1777.

And there you have the reason for her fame. For Dolly, it was claimed, had been the very last person to speak Cornish, and *only* Cornish.

Long after her burial in Paul Parish Church, Mousehole, Prince Louis Bonaparte, (a keen amateur historian) and the vicar of the church, John Garrett, devised the present epitaph, which is set into the churchyard wall. With great diplomacy they used the phrase 'said to have been the last person who conversed in the ancient Cornish language.' It includes the injunction 'Honour thy father and thy mother' etc. (Exod. xx.12) in both English and Cornish:

Gwra perth de taz ha de mam mal de dythiow bethenz
hyr war an tyr neb an arleth de dew ryes dees.

DORA RUSSELL

1894–1986
(née Black)
Lived: Carn Voel, Porthcurno

We cannot know what may be the ultimate fate of ourselves or of so much of that universe towards which, day and night, eternally we gaze, longing with the whole of our being to know and understand more. So great a thing it is to be alive, to be human. (Dora Russell, *The Tamarisk Tree*, Vol. 3, 1985)

Dora Black was born at Thornton Heath, Surrey. She read modern languages at Girton College, Cambridge, obtaining a first class degree in 1915. In 1921 she married Bertrand Russell. They had two children and founded a progressive school, Beacon Hill, in Sussex. They were divorced in the 1930s.

An enthusiastic and indefatigable campaigner for birth control, women's rights and world peace, Dora created the Women's Caravan for Peace in 1958. Among her publications are *Hypathia: or*

Women of Knowledge (1925), *In Defence of Children* (1932) and three volumes of autobiography, *The Tamarisk Tree* (1977, 1981 and 1985).

For over sixty years Dora Russell's home was in Cornwall.

Blue, white, grey are the clouds,
And patches of grey and silver are made on the sea
And paths of blue and pearl for the ships to go.

Blue, white, grey is the house
I have made on the hilltop,
Where the clouds shall go over and winds shall blow
And we shall gaze on the sea.
Children and lawns and flowers shall blossom about us.
When we die, may we sleep in love;
Perhaps in the winds our thoughts will speak to our children.
(Dora Russell, *The Tamarisk Tree*, Vol. 1, 1977)

SMUGGLERS' ACCOMPLICES

Lowland Point, near St Keverne

The trouble with smuggling is that unless those concerned were actually caught, tried and punished, no one really 'talked'. One is left with tantalizing fragments, brief references and half-truths.

Women, such as Nancy Cox, Betsy Matthews and Bessie Bussow, were often deeply involved as accomplices. Sometimes they owned, or ran, 'kiddleywinks', (imagine a very small, very local pub, where everyone knows everyone else and turns to look when a stranger walks in, and you have a good idea of a kiddleywink), and from these they gave essential help to smugglers attempting to land their illegal haul. They signalled all-clears and other messages by lighting fires; they knew when the coast was clear, the tide was right; and, more than anything else, they knew how to keep their mouths shut.

Bessie had a cove named after her, Nancy a field, and Betsy Matthews a rock, called 'Betsy's Cliff'. Betsy lived near St Keverne, on the Lizard.

FLORENCE WILMOT THOMAS

1873–1966
Lived: Penlee,
St Just-in-Penwith

Florence Thomas, of St Just-in-Penwith, was the first woman to be enrolled as a member of the Women's Institute (WI) in Cornwall.

She started the first Institute in 1918 at St Just and devoted much of her life to its aims and activities, becoming, as she said herself, 'President *and* Secretary for a long time'.

During the First World War Florence was Commandant of the Red Cross; during the Second World War, as leader of the Women's Voluntary Services, she helped to organize the distribution and welfare of London evacuees in Cornwall.

Miss Thomas, not surprisingly, did not marry – she had far too much to do. Apart from her interest in the WI, she became Chairman of the Governors of Penzance Girls' Grammar School. She represented St Just on the County Council for nine years, was organizer of the St Just branch of the County Library, Chairman of their Horticultural Show Committee and Leader of the St Just Church Sunday School.

She died in 1966, aged ninety-three.

ANNE TRENEER

1891–1966
Born: Gorran

My brothers say they brought me up in the wheelbarrow, and that this accounts for certain bumps in my forehead and general scrappy appearance. When I was small they used to tell me that old Mrs Tucker brought me one winter night in a potato sack and left me on the front step; and that I squalled so loud that my father said to my mother, 'For God's sake bring the little devil in and see if she'll stop that noise'. So in I came and stayed. (Anne Treneer, *School House in the Wind*, 1944)

Anne Treneer was born at Gorran in Cornwall, where her father was the headmaster of the school. With four elder brothers she grew up both independent and adventurous.

When she was ten the family moved to Caerhays, three miles away, where the School House was less windblown, and where Anne was equally happy. She went to school at St Austell, trained as a teacher at Truro, went to college at Liverpool and later to Lady Margaret Hall, Oxford.

Anne Treneer wrote a life of the Cornish scientist, Sir Humphry Davy, *The Mercurial Chemist* (1963). She also wrote poetry, short stories and historical studies for various periodicals, including J. C. Trewin's *West Country Magazine*. Her three volumes of autobiography are *School House in the Wind*, *Cornish Years* and *A Stranger in the Midlands*.

LADY VYVYAN

1886–1976
(née Clara Coltman Rogers)
Lived: Trelowarren House, Mawgan, Lizard Peninsula

Yet now, after all my wanderings, and wonderings, what knowledge or what understanding have I gained that I may presume to share . . . ? Only this.

It is not necessary to travel before you can stand quietly and allow yourself to be stabbed through and through by the beauty and the mystery of some growing thing. Whenever you see a tuft of moss in a crevice, or a tree habitually looking up to the sky, or a daffodil, nodding and erect while it stands as herald of the spring in the early days of March, you will know that, so long as the moss, the flower and the tree are with

us, there is hope for mankind in this troubled world. (C. C. Vyvyan, *Letters from a Cornish Garden*, 1972)

Clara Coltman Rogers was born in Australia of a Cornish mother; at the age of two she arrived in Cornwall, and was brought up there. An unconventional and restless young woman, she worked at the University Settlement in Southwark, London, and attended the London School of Economics, where she took her degree. After this she began a very personal, almost private exploration, the study of places, people and everything that grew.

In 1926 she travelled up the Rat River, over the Divide and into Klondyke Country (NW America), with her friend Gwen Dorrien-Smith. In 1929 she married Colonel Sir Courtenay Vyvyan, tenth Baronet and owner of Trelowarren House on the Lizard Peninsula in Cornwall. After his death in 1941, she devoted herself to the estate, successfully running a market garden to pay off a mortgage.

Lady Vyvyan continued to travel and, aged sixty-seven, she walked four hundred miles along the Rhone Valley from its source to the Mediterranean delta, and then described the experience in *Down the Rhone on Foot* (1955). She always returned to Trelowarren, to its beautiful grounds and the 'Lady's Garden' and, in one of the best of her twenty books, *The Old Place* (1952), she told its story.

Trelowarren House, Lizard Peninsula, home of Clara Vyvyan

ANNE WALKE

c. 1888–1965
(née Fearon)
The Jesus Chapel, Truro Cathedral, Cornwall

Crucifixion in Truro Cathedral

Ann Fearon studied at the Chelsea School of Art and the London School of Art. After her marriage to Bernard Walke she moved to Cornwall:

We lived in Polruan. Polruan is a little seaport across the harbour from Fowey . . . Here Annie Walke had a studio in a sail-loft overlooking the harbour. (Bernard Walke)

Her husband was curate at the church of St Saviour on the Hill, but he was unconventional, always getting into scrapes, and not at all approved of by traditional church officials. When he was offered the living of St Hilary he decided to accept, and he and Annie lived there for the next twenty years. Annie continued to work and, when the church at St Hilary was redecorated, she painted an altar piece representing St Joan in one of the aisles.

Annie moved to Mevagissey after her husband's death and continued to paint well into old age.

Much of her work is privately owned in Cornwall, but she painted the Crucifixion in the Jesus Chapel, Truro Cathedral, and in 1985 she was included in the Newlyn Orion Exhibition, 'Painting in Newlyn 1900–30'.

VERONICA WHALL

1887–1967
King Arthur's Hall,
Tintagel

Although other examples of her work exist in Devon, Gloucester, Leicester and as far away as New Zealand, Veronica Whall's major achievement as a stained-glass artist is to be found in King Arthur's Hall at Tintagel, Cornwall.

Commissioned by F. T. Glasscock, the custard millionaire who initiated the project, she worked on the windows for his hall from 1929 to 1933, and eventually all seventy-three were complete. In her own words:

> These windows are designed to illustrate the story of King Arthur and the Fellowship of the Round Table in connection with the Quest of the Holy Grail, taking only those incidents and characters which emphasise the beautiful symbolic meaning underlying the legend.

Astonishingly, Veronica's name in connection with her work seems to have fallen into almost complete oblivion. To give her, therefore, some long overdue recognition: Veronica was the daughter of a well-known Victorian stained-glass artist, Christopher Whall. Born in London, she was trained and influenced by her father and also attended classes at the Central School of Arts and Crafts. When her father died she and her brother took over and ran the studio in London. Veronica did most of the designing, including a memorial window to her father in Gloucester Cathedral. Then came the commission for the Hall in Tintagel.

Unfortunately, Frederick Thomas Glasscock did not seem to appreciate the value of her work and, although she later took him to court, Veronica never received proper compensation. She was always of a nervous disposition and the disappointment and controversy is thought to have severely affected her health.

Nevertheless, her beautiful windows remain, their glowing colours giving fascination to a Hall that, without them, would be merely quite ordinary.

THE WIVES AND YOUNG WOMEN'S WINDOWS OF ST NEOT

St Neot Church, St Neot

Situated on the southern edge of Bodmin Moor, the town of St Neot is the proud possesser of a fifteenth-century church with beautiful stained-glass windows.

Dating from the early sixteenth century, these windows were paid for by the principal local families of the parish. It is thought that when the vicar ran out of families he turned to public subscription, for in the north aisle, one finds one window donated by 'wives' and another by 'young women'. Both windows are particularly charming, as they include a row of little kneeling figures along their lower edge – each one an individual portrait of the donors.

Veronica Whall's stained-glass windows in King Arthur's Hall, Tintagel

VIRGINIA WOOLF

1882–1941
(née Stephen)
Godrevy Lighthouse, off
Godrevy Point

We are between Gurnard's Head and
Zennor. I see the nose of the Gurnard
from my window. We step into the
June sunshine past mounds of newly
sprung gorse, bright yellow and
smelling of nuts. (Letter from
Virginia Woolf to Saxon
Sydney-Turner)

Virginia Woolf, novelist and
essayist, was born in London but
she spent most of her childhood
holidays at Talland House in
St Ives. Later she wove her
impressions and feelings about
Cornwall into *To The Lighthouse*
(1927). Of this novel she wrote in
May 1925 'This is going to be
fairly short; to have father's
character done complete in it; and
mother's; and St Ives; and
childhood; and all the usual things

I try to put in – life, death, etc.'
(The Diary of Virginia Woolf,
vol. 3, 1980)
    Her affection for Cornwall was
such that her husband, Leonard
Woolf, took her back there in an
attempt to alleviate the despair of
her recurring depressions:

> As the final cure, we wandered round
> St Ives and crept into the garden of
> Talland House and in the dusk
> Virginia peered through the
> ground-floor windows to see the
> ghosts of her childhood. (Leonard
> Woolf, *Downhill All the Way*, 1967)

No permanent cure was ever
found, and one of the finest and
most sensitive writers of the early
twentieth century drowned herself
in the River Ouse in Sussex.

Godrevy Lighthouse

DOROTHY YGLESIAS

1891–1980

PHYLLIS YGLESIAS

1892–1977

Mousehole Wild Bird Hospital and Sanctuary

The collection box in the garden of the Mousehole Wild Bird Hospital and Sanctuary

Friday, 14th March 1967. The papers called it Black Friday, the day of the Black Tide and the Black Death . . . It was the day the oil from the huge wrecked tanker 'Torrey Canyon' first came to the Cornish beaches and, for us at the R.S.P.C.A. Wild Birds' Hospital in Mousehole, it was the day Operation Bird Wash began. (Dorothy Yglesias, *In Answer to the Cry*, 1978)

After the *Torrey Canyon* disaster in 1967, Dorothy Yglesias and her sister Phyllis became national heroines. Eight thousand oiled birds were received at a little wild birds' hospital and sanctuary, founded by these two sisters in Mousehole.

Dorothy and Phyllis (or 'Pog' as she was known all her life) were

born in London. They visited Mousehole in Cornwall for their holidays and in 1925 they moved there permanently, living in a house they had built, called Cherry Orchard. Pog, who carved in wood, moved her studio from a net loft near the harbour to a wooden hut near the house.

In 1928 a jackdaw with a broken wing was brought to them, and Pog looked after him. Gradually both sisters became more and more interested in bird life. They began to take in injured birds of every kind, building runs, pools and homes for their ever-increasing patients until they had established their Hospital and Sanctuary.

By 1945 the Royal Society for the Prevention of Cruelty to Animals (RSPCA) were interested enough not only to give financial aid, but to help with repairs and rebuilding. Dorothy and Pog moved from Cherry Orchard to Green Hedges and, in 1960, the RSPCA took over responsibility. The Yglesias sisters continued to take an active interest and Dorothy published her best-selling book, *The Cry of a Bird* (1962). Then came the *Torrey Canyon* disaster.

In 1975 the RSPCA decided to close down the Hospital, as part of an economy drive; Dorothy and Pog, both in their eighties, managed to keep it open with the help of a local committee. After their deaths, the Hospital was still struggling for survival in 1984. Whether it continues to exist or not, the closing words of Dorothy's second book, *In Answer to the Cry* (1978), should be remembered:

Now as I come to the end of my book the cries of the oiled birds can be heard yet again. The giant tanker 'Amoco Cadiz' has this week run on to the rocks off Brittany spilling out twice as much oil as did the 'Torrey Canyon' . . . What can be done? How can atonement be made? The answer must be the concern of all and everyone of us.

DEVON

JUDITH ACKLAND

1892–1971
Lived: 'The Cabin', Bucks Mills

At Bucks Mills, near Bideford, just before the narrow road drops steeply towards the sea, there is a small, solid-looking cottage. It is not at all pretty, but has a peculiar attraction of its own and is called 'The Cabin'. This was the home for many years of two artists, Judith Ackland and her friend, Mary Stella Edwards.

Judith Ackland was born in Bideford. She began to study art there but then moved to London where she met fellow-student Mary and they began their lifelong friendship.

From the early 1920s they began to use The Cabin as a base. Judith Ackland's first exhibition of watercolours was held at Bideford in 1922. Five years later one of her pictures, *The Tarn* was shown at the Royal Academy in London. Judith was primarily a water-colour painter, but in 1945 she became interested in making models and devised an unusual method involving cottonwool, which she registered under the name *Jackanda*. The figures she made in this way were often based on famous paintings, such as her *Lady in Blue*, after *The Parisian Girl* by Renoir, and *David Garrick and his Wife*, after Hogarth.

In 1949 the two friends worked together on their first diorama (a miniature three-dimensional scene, in which models of figures are set in a background). Their dioramas proved so popular that in 1954 Windsor Borough Council commissioned seven for an exhibition on local history.

Judith Ackland died at Bideford in 1971.

MIRIAM ADAMS

1781–1858
Buried: St Andrew's Church, Ashburton

The news of the Battle of Waterloo and the defeat of Napoleon in June 1815 had reached almost everyone in Britain within a fortnight. In the little town of Ashburton in Devon the news was broken by the local postwoman, Miriam Adams. It was a dramatic highlight of her career.

For most of her life Miriam did the rounds of Ashburton, riding on her donkey, Betsy, and accompanied for many years by her dog, Traveller. When she died a number of the townswomen clubbed together and provided a gravestone and inscription for her.

The gravestone still stands by the side of a path in the churchyard of St Andrew's. The inscription is now very faint, but reads:

This tablet is erected to the memory of Miriam Adams who for forty-four years discharged her responsible duties of letter-carrier to the Post Office in this town with uniform cheerfulness and strict fidelity. She died Oct 12th 1858 Aged 77.

Judith Ackland: her home at 'The Cabin', Bucks Mills, near Bideford

PRUDENCE BALDWIN

c. 1660
Plaque: Dean Prior
Church

Robert Herrick, the seventeenth-century poet, was the vicar of Dean Prior in Devon from 1629 to 1647, and from 1662 to 1674. He never married, but was lovingly tended by his servant and housekeeper, Prudence Baldwin. When she died, he wrote a charming epitaph for her, which was later engraved on copper and placed on the tower screen of Dean Prior Church:

> In this little urn is laid
> Prewdence Baldwin, once my maid,
> From whose happy spark here let
> Spring the purple violet.

THE BIDEFORD WITCHES

d. 1682
Hanged: Heavitree,
Exeter

> Now listen to my Song, good People all,
> And I shall tell what lately did befall
> At Exeter a place in Devonshire,
> The like whereof of late you nere did hear
> (seventeenth-century ballad)

At the assizes held at Exeter in 1682, three old women, Mary Trembles, Susanna Edwards and Temperance Lloyd, were accused of witchcraft. They all came from Bideford. All three confessed, were found guilty and were hanged on 25 August of that year. A ballad of seventeen verses was composed to celebrate the occasion.

Three hundred years later, it is very difficult to understand the strength of the emotions that made their pathetic deaths inevitable. Popular feeling ran so high that it would have been a brave judge indeed who would have dared to acquit them.

> Having Familiars always at their Beck,
> Their wicked Rage on Mortals for to wreck;
> It being proved they used Wicked Charms,
> To Murder Men, and bring about sad harms

The three old women not only confessed to supernatural abilities and knowledge of the devil, but even volunteered further evidence: Temperance Lloyd admitted to having caused several shipwrecks.

Fifty years later the act which made witchcraft a capital offence was removed from the statute book.

CICELY BONVILLE

b. 1460
Ottery St Mary Parish
Church

Cicely, a member of the Bonville family, the owners of Shute Barton in Devon, was probably born there. Orphaned at an early age, she inherited the estate and in 1476 married Thomas Grey, Marquis of Dorset. An exceptionally wealthy woman, she eventually gave birth to fifteen children and was the great-grandmother of Lady Jane Grey.

She is remembered for her generous contributions to various churches on her estates, particularly one that has been described as 'the loveliest in Devon', the church at Ottery St Mary. Cicely's money provided the north aisle, known as the Dorset aisle, with its fan-vaulted roof, hanging bosses and angel corbels.

ANNA ELIZA BRAY

1790–1883
(née Kempe)
Lived: The Vicarage,
Tavistock

In 1818 Anna Kempe married Charles Stothard, an artist. Three years later, Charles fell off a ladder while drawing a stained-glass window and died of his injuries. Some time after this Anna married the Reverend Bray, vicar of the parish church of St Eustachius, Tavistock, in Devon.

Mrs Bray, pretty, vivacious and highly strung, took to writing romances. Many of her novels were based on local families, such as the Trelawneys, the Pomeroys and the Courtenays, but the book which really brought her to everyone's notice was *The Borders of the Tamar and Tavy*, published

Cicely Bonville: Ottery St Mary Parish Church

in three volumes in 1836. Occasionally inaccurate, always enthusiastic and entertaining, it is packed with fascinating information on the area. History, geology and botany jostle with legends, superstitions, witches, pixies, ghosts and murders.

Mrs Bray is also known for her discovery of Mary Colling (q.v.) servant of a local family, who wrote unusually good poetry.

Anna Bray died aged ninety-three. Her autobiography was published posthumously.

65

BUCKLAND CLOCK

Buckland-in-the-Moor Church

The Clock on the church at Buckland-in-the-Moor in Devon has no numerals on its face, instead it reads, 'My dear mother'. There is no official explanation for this charming deviation, but one story told is that a local boy, a sailor, was believed to be lost at sea. His mother refused to accept his death and kept a candle lit in her cottage window every night. She also left food on the table before she went to bed.

Her son *did* return and, touched by his mother's love and faith, he paid to have the clock erected on the church, after her death.

Buckland Clock at Buckland-in-the-Moor Church

DAME GEORGIANA BULLER

1883–1953
Founded: St Loyes, Exeter

All who have had any connection with St Loyes will be aware how great an influence Dame Georgiana Buller had on all departments of the College life and how greatly all who knew her mourn her death. We owe our origin and our development to her vision and her efforts . . . Dame Georgiana was a master of strategy and tactics, with powers of persuasion which few could resist – she would never take no for an answer. (St Loyes Annual Report, 1953)

Georgiana Buller founded St Loyes College for the Training and Rehabilitation of the Disabled, Exeter, in 1937.

Born in Devon, Georgiana was the only daughter of General Buller, and seems to have inherited all the qualities that made him an exemplary soldier.

In 1914 she established and administered a Voluntary Aid Hospital at Exeter and, when the War Office took over, she was appointed Administrator – the only woman to hold such a post. In 1920 she was created DBE in recognition of her achievements. Between the two World Wars Dame Georgiana became interested in the rehabilitation of the physically disabled and, convinced that with suitable training disabled men and women could take their place in the community, she conceived the idea of a residential college. St Loyes was the result.

Portrait of Dame
Georgiana Buller

THE SKELETON OF CHAMBERCOMBE MANOR

c. 1695
Chambercombe Manor,
Ilfracombe

In 1865 the tenant of Chambercombe Manor near Ilfracombe was carrying out various repairs to the property. Noticing a discrepancy in the design of the old house, he investigated further and discovered a small, sealed room. Inside the room was an ancient bedstead and on the bed lay the skeleton of a woman.

It is quite clear that no one will ever know exactly who she was, although all the evidence points to an incident in 1695 when a ship was wrecked off the coast near Ilfracombe. A wealthy young woman was rescued from the wreck and secretly taken to

Chambercombe Manor. She died there.

Was she murdered for her jewellery? Did she die of her injuries – and was then stripped of her jewels? Was she, as some have thought, actually Kate Oatway, daughter of the owner of Chambercombe at the time, or a complete stranger? Does she, as some claim, still haunt the beautiful old house, smiling happily and wrapped in a grey cloak?

Whoever she was, she was buried anonymously in Ilfracombe churchyard. Chambercombe is well worth a visit, even if one is not in a mood for solving mysteries.

BEATRICE CHASE (OLIVE KATHARINE PARR)

1874–1955
Buried: St Pancras Churchyard,
Widecombe-in-the-Moor

I hate July more than any month in the year. It's so fliey, so thunderous, so cloudy and misty and vaporous, so downright tame, with its monotonous greens all burnt to the same tint. If Dartmoor can ever look ugly it's in July. (Beatrice Chase, *Devon and Heaven*, 1925)

Beatrice Chase, founder of the 'Crusade of White Knights and Ladies', sole organizer of the 'Crusade for Chastity' and prolific popular writer, lived at Venton House, Widecombe-in-the-Moor, for over fifty years. She also owned a Catholic chapel there.

Born at Harrow, she was educated at the Convent of the Holy Child in Cavendish Square, London. Early in the First World War her fiancé died in action, and it was said that she never really recovered from the shock.

Among her many novels were *Lady Agatha: A Romance of Tintagel*, *The Little Cardinal*, and *Lady Avis Trewithen: A Romance of Dartmoor*. Her books on the area, such as *Through a Dartmoor Window*, combined a strong religious element with local characterization. In the *Times* obituary (headed 'Miss O. K. Parr') this comment appeared: 'For the fastidious her writing is too luscious and extravagant but it appealed to a large majority that regarded her as the apostle of beauty and purity.'

Beatrice Chase sometimes misjudged her audience, and when she wrote an extraordinary diatribe *Woman's Emancipation (By One Who Does Not Want It)*, she found that she had to publish and distribute the booklet herself:

Like the Marquise who ran, laughing up the steps of the guillotine rather than save her life by kissing Robespierre, I have never hesitated, through fear of consequences, to act according to what I consider principle. (Introduction to the booklet)

She was passionate about the preservation of Dartmoor and became Vice-President of the South-Western branch of the League Against Cruel Sports. When she died she left instructions that she should be buried in a field, clothed in her Dominican Tertiary habit, but her executors decided that her wish could not be fulfilled. Miss Olive Katharine Parr, Beatrice Chase, was conventionally buried in the churchyard of Widecombe-in-the-Moor.

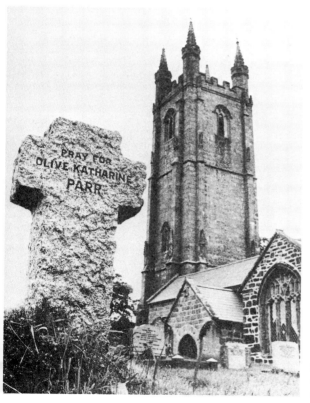

Beatrice Chase's grave in the churchyard of Widecombe-in-the-Moor

ROSALIE CHICHESTER

1865–1949

Lived: Arlington Court, between Barnstaple and Lynmouth

Memorial to Rosalie Chichester by the side of the lake at Arlington Court

Miss Chichester was born at Arlington Court, home of the Chichesters for centuries, and lived there all her life. When her father, Sir Bruce Chichester, died in 1881, he left a heavily mortgaged estate.

Between them, his widow and his daughter, Rosalie, spent the next fifty years paying off debts and working to preserve the house, its contents and its beautiful grounds. When Rosalie Chichester died in 1949, she made a gift of the whole estate to the National Trust. It was opened to the public in 1952 and should definitely be visited if one is in the area.

The house is a treasure-trove for avid collectors, filled with model ships, sea shells, pewter and paintings. Every room is indelibly stamped with the taste of its last private owner and her family.

The grounds are extensive, with a nature trail leading to the lake, duck sanctuary and heronry. By the side of the lake is a stone urn on a pedestal: 'Here lies Rosalie Caroline Chichester of Arlington, 1865–1949'.

AGATHA CHRISTIE

1890–1976
(née Miller)

Lived: Torquay, Devon

Agatha Christie was born in Torquay, Devon. In her *Autobiography* (1977) she described the house she loved so dearly:

It was an ordinary enough villa, not in the fashionable part of Torquay . . . but at the other end of the town, the older part of Tor Mohun. At that time the road in which it was situated led almost at once into rich Devon country, with lanes and fields. The name of the house was Ashfield and it has been my home, off and on, nearly all my life.

When she was over seventy – and was told that her old home had been sold and was about to be demolished – she tried to buy Ashfield back. It was too late. A new estate was built on the site. Agatha married Archibald Christie in 1914. In 1920 her first detective story, *The Mysterious Affair at Styles*, was published, conceived, so she claimed, while working in a dispensary:

Since I was surrounded by poisons, perhaps it was natural that death by poisoning should be the method I selected.

She finished the last half of the book while on holiday in a hotel at Hay Tor, on Dartmoor, introducing for the first time her detective hero, Hercule Poirot.

Agatha Christie divorced her first husband in 1928, and married Max Mallowan, the archaeologist, two years later.

It is said that the only books to have sold better than hers are the Bible and Shakespeare's plays. She became a very wealthy woman and was honoured by being made Dame of the British Empire in 1971.

She died at Wallingford in Oxfordshire, having never forgotten her birthplace in Torquay:

I go back to that always in my mind. Ashfield.
'O ma chère maison, mon nid, mo
gîte
Le passé l'habite . . . O! ma chère
maison'
How much that means. When I dream . . . it is always Ashfield.
(*Autobiography*, 1977)

MARY, LADY CHUDLEIGH

1656–1710
(née Lee)
Buried: Higher Ashton
Church

Ladies,
The Love of Truth, the tender Regard I have for your Honour, joyn'd with a just Indignation to see you so unworthily us'd makes me assume the Confidence of imploying my Pen in your Service. (Lady Mary Chudleigh, 1701)

Lady Mary, a very early 'feminist', was married to Sir George Chudleigh of Place Barton, Higher Ashton, Devon. Although she had three children her marriage was not at all happy and, after her daughter's death, she retreated into what seemed to be a resigned acceptance of her situation.

Then one day, when in her forties, she went to church as usual and sat through a long sermon on Conjugal Duty, preached by a Mr Sprint. After the service, seething with anger, she went home, sat down and began to write a long poem. It was called *The Ladies Defence, or The Bride-Woman's Counsellor Answer'd*, and was published in 1701. Written in the form of a dialogue, four characters fiercely argue about the status of women in society. Three of them are men and one a woman, Melissa. Lady Mary left no doubt as to whose side she was on:

Melissa: Must men command, and we alone obey
As if designed for Arbitrary Sway:
Born petty Monarchs, and, like Homer's Gods,
See all subjected to their haughty nods?
Narcissus-like, you your own Graces view,
Think none deserve to be admired but you.

The Ladies Defence caused quite a commotion in public and, no doubt, some trouble at home. When her publisher wanted to reprint, the author refused her consent. He issued it anyway.

Two years later Lady Mary Chudleigh produced *Poems on Several Occasions* and, just before her death, *Essay on Several Subjects*. She was buried in the church at Higher Ashton, with no monument or inscription.

Tis hard we should be by the Men despis'd
Yet kept from knowing what wou'd make us priz'd;
Debarr'd from Knowledge, banish'd from the Schools,
And with the utmost Industry bred Fools.
(*The Ladies Defence*)

ANN CLARK

1656–1733
Buried: St George's
Church, Tiverton

Ann Clark, midwife, of Tiverton, died aged seventy-seven and was buried with this verse on her tombstone:

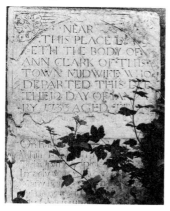

On harmless babes I did attend,
Whilst I on earth my life did spend;
To help the helpless in their need,
I ready was with care and speed.

Many from pain my hands did free,
But none from death could rescue me;
My glass is run, my hour is past,
And yours is coming all too fast.

The Reverend Richard Polwhele carefully noted her unusual epitaph in his *History of Devonshire* (1797–1806). No doubt he was also impressed by the fact that, during her career, Ann had delivered over five thousand babies.

This interesting gravestone can now be found against the northside (outer) wall of St George's Church, Tiverton.

MARY COLLING

1805–?
Born and lived:
Tavistock

A group of Monkies and two Apes
Had spent the day in gathering
grapes;
At eve, beneath an oak they sat,
And pass'd some hours in friendly
chat;
When lo! in course of conversation,
The Apes both made an observation,
That 'twould be right some grapes to
spare,
And for cold winter's wants prepare.
We've got a cave, said they, you
know,
Where you may all your hoards
bestow
And on our word you may rely;
Fear not our honesty to try.
The Monkies, one and all, combined
To thank them for their offer kind;
And brought, without delay, their
grapes
To these supposed kind-hearted
Apes.
But when cold winter frowns, behold
The Monkies, shivering with the
cold,
All sought the Apes their grapes to
gain,
Not thinking all their toil was vain.
At last, with many a surly flout,
The consequential cheats walk'd out,
And thus address'd the clamorous
crew:
Pray, what's the cause of this ado?
Tease us no more about your grapes;
We are not worse than other Apes;
And to obtain, and ne'er repay,
Is quite the fashion of the day.
(Mary Maria Colling, *Fables, and
other pieces in Verse*, 1831)

Mary Colling, born in Tavistock,
went into service with a Mrs
Hughes when she was fourteen,
and remained with the family after
Mrs Hughes' death. She eventually
became their housekeeper.
Mrs Bray (q.v.) the vicar's wife,
noticed Mary at church and,
feeling that there was something
different about her, made efforts to
find out more. She discovered that
Mary wrote poetry and that much
of it was exceptionally good.
Mrs Bray took Mary under her
wing, encouraged her, and wrote
to her friend, Robert Southey, the
poet, about her protégée.
In 1831 Mary's fables were
published, interspersed with Mrs
Bray's letters to Robert Southey.
Some of Mrs Bray's comments,
although well-meant, sound a little
patronizing but are the only
description of Mary that we have:

She has the Devonshire accent, but
not coarsely; and, though a perfect
country girl in every thing – in her
smile, her cap, her little straw bonnet
and her curtsy – yet there is nothing
vulgar about her.

Nevertheless, to Mrs Bray must
go the credit of having discovered
and published the work of an
interesting and unusual minor
poet.

HANNAH COWLEY

1743–1809
(née Parkhouse)
Buried: St George's
Churchyard, Tiverton
(exact site unknown)

Hannah Parkhouse, the daughter
of a bookseller, was born in
Tiverton, Devon. At the age of
twenty-five she married Mr
Cowley and had several children.
They lived in London, and it is said
that Hannah, having been to the
theatre one night, sat down the
next day and wrote her first play,
The Runaway. This was first
produced at Drury Lane in 1776
and was praised by David Garrick.
Two more plays followed: *The
Belle's Stratagem* (1780) and *A
Bold Stroke for a Husband* (1783).
This shy, retiring woman from
Devonshire, who 'never witnessed
a first performance of one of her
own plays', wrote at great speed.
Fortunately the (anonymous)

author of the preface to *The Work
of Hannah Cowley* left a vivid
description of Hannah's approach

She was always much pleased with
the description of Michael Angelo
making marble fly around him, as
he was chiselling with the utmost
swiftness, that he might shape,
however roughly, his whole design in
unity with one clear conception. If
she found she could not proceed
swiftly, she gave up what she had
undertaken.

Not long after her husband's
death, Hannah retired to Tiverton.
She died there in 1809 and was
buried in St George's churchyard.
A fragment of her tombstone was
found there in 1968 and is now in
the Tiverton Museum.

E. M. DELAFIELD (MRS DASHWOOD)

1890–1943
(née de la Pasture)
Lived: Cullompton

Not quite thirty years ago, the readers of *Time and Tide* were enjoying successive instalments of a minor classic: *The Diary of a Provincial Lady*, by E. M. Delafield. Poor Provincial Lady, she had a dreadful time of it. Her children let her down with a wallop in company; her husband greeted her profoundest thoughts with impenetrable silence; her bank-manager was unsympathetic; her clothes were somehow always ill-assorted; whenever she arranged a picnic or went to a tennis party it rained, icily. (Honor Croome in *Time and Tide*, 1959)

Edmée Elizabeth Monica de la Pasture, the eldest daughter of Count Henry de la Pasture of Monmouthshire, married Arthur Dashwood in 1919. She had already published her first novel, *Zella Sees Herself* (1917) had served as a VAD, and been offered an appointment in Bristol with the Ministry of National Service. After her marriage she spent two years in the Malay States, had two children and settled in Devon.

As 'E. M. Delafield', she wrote forty books, contributed to *Punch*, *Time and Tide*, and made a number of broadcasts for women on the radio. Her most popular book, *The Diary of a Provincial Lady*, was published in 1931 and led to sequels such as *Thank Heaven Fasting*, *The Provincial Lady Goes Further* and *The Provincial Lady in War*.

Mrs Dashwood was greatly liked in the village of Cullompton where she and her family made their home for so many years, and where she died in 1943 at the age of fifty-two.

DOROTHY DODDERIDGE

1582–1614
(née Bampfield)
Tomb: Exeter Cathedral

As when a curious clocke is out of frame
A workman takes in peeces small the same
And me(n)dinge what amisse is to be found
The same rejoynes and makes it trewe and sound
So God this Ladie into two partes tooke
Too soone her soule her mortall corse forsooke
(Dodderidge Memorial, Exeter Cathedral)

Dorothy, the wife of John Dodderidge, Solicitor-General and Judge in the reign of James I, died in childbirth. Little is known of her personally, but a visit to her tomb on the north side of the Lady Chapel in Exeter Cathedral is well worthwhile. The effigy shows her lying sideways, resting on her right elbow and looking rather uncomfortable, but it is her clothes that deserve close inspection. Dorothy wears an interesting head-dress, a ruff and a beautiful flower-patterned dress, which has a lace collar and cuffs. For those who enjoy studying the history of dress, this is an excellent example of early seventeenth-century costume.

Dorothy Dodderidge's tomb in Exeter Cathedral

DOROTHY ELMHIRST

1887–1968
(née Whitney)
Founded: Dartington Hall, Totnes

Dorothy Elmhirst and her husband founded the well-known experimental school at Dartington Hall, near Totnes in Devon.

Born in Washington, USA, Dorothy was the daughter of William Collins Whitney, Secretary of the US Navy at the time, and a very wealthy man. Her mother died when she was only six years old and Dorothy, well-educated, well-travelled and well-off, married Willard Straight in 1911. Seven years later her husband died of influenza and she was left a widow and the mother of two children, aged only thirty-one.

Two years later, in 1920, she met Leonard Elmhirst, an Englishman studying agriculture at Cornell University. Leonard became secretary to the Indian poet and philosopher, Rabindranath Tagore, and helped him to found the Institute of Rural Reconstruction near Surul in West Bengal. Dorothy became more and more attracted, not only to Leonard himself but to his ideas on education and, although he had to propose to her several times, she finally accepted him. They were married at Westbury, in the USA, in 1925.

Almost immediately the Elmhirsts moved to England,

where they planned to open a school, and soon bought the old manor of Dartington Hall in Devon. By the end of 1926 they had moved in, Dorothy had given birth to their first child, and the first six pupils had arrived.

The school was run on 'free' experimental lines and, although there were difficulties and problems, the number of pupils rose to twenty-five within three years. Among those who attended Dartington in its early years were three grandsons of Sigmund Freud, Aldous Huxley's son Matthew and two of Bertrand Russell's children.

Dorothy, a shy and retiring woman, was often homesick. She and her husband were sometimes misunderstood by the locals who were suspicious and distrustful of these very wealthy and extremely unconventional 'foreigners'. Nevertheless, the Elmhirsts persevered, and the school was for many years a great success.

Dorothy herself was particularly involved in the dance, drama and pottery classes at the school. She was an enthusiastic art-collector, loved gardening, and threw herself into every new project with great energy. She died at Dartington and her ashes were scattered in the garden there.

MARIA FOOTE

1797–1867
(Countess of Harrington)
Born: Plymouth

Maria was born in Plymouth where her father managed a theatre. At about the age of fourteen she played Juliet in Shakespeare's *Romeo and Juliet* there, but not long after this the family moved to Exeter where her father ran a hotel. Maria continued her stage career and in 1814 appeared as Amanthis in Mrs Inchbald's *The Child of Nature* at Covent Garden, London. She was asked to join the company, playing Miranda in *The Tempest*.

Maria Foote was never considered a great actress, but she was talented and very beautiful,

and her love-life caused more than a flutter of interest. She had two children by a Colonel Berkeley who, it is said, promised to marry her. The marriage did not take place and Maria later sued a Mr Haynes for breach of promise. She won her case and Mr Haynes had to pay her three thousand pounds in damages.

In 1831 Maria married Charles Stanhope, eighth Earl of Harrington, and, with this dramatic and, one can't help feeling, triumphant flourish, retired from the stage.

ISABELLA DE FORTIBUS

d. 1292
(Countess of Devon)
Countess Wear: between
Topsham and Exeter

On Farway Common, near Honiton, three parishes meet, and there were incessant disputes as to the boundary. Isabella decided it thus. She flung her ring into the air, and where it fell that was to be the point of junction for Gittisham, Farway, and Honiton. The spot is still called 'Ring-in-the-Mere'. Such at least is the local legend accounting for the name. (S. Baring-Gould, *Devon*, 1899)

Isabella was quite capable of deciding minor issues in such an arbitrary way. On her brother's death she inherited the estates of the Earls of Devon, and became Countess of Devon and a very powerful woman – a position she quite obviously enjoyed.

One of her most arrogant actions has never been forgotten in the history of Exeter and Topsham. In 1284, having quarrelled with the city authorities of Exeter, she decided to punish them by damming the river below the city, thus effectively cutting off the passage of ships and trade. Topsham, sitting smugly on the right side of the dam, became a flourishing port with, eventually, a quay and a Custom House. It took over two hundred years before a canal was built from the centre of Exeter to a point below Isabella's dam. This place is *still* called Countess Wear.

MARIA SUSANNAH GIBBONS

1841–1900
Lived: Vicarsmead
(privately owned) East
Budleigh

First we must say of whom 'We Donkeys' consist. *Seniores Priores*, an 'unprotected female' of a certain age, and yet hardly 'unprotected', because the second member of our party is a handsome black dog, named 'Romulus', that will guard and protect the whole cavalcade, and though the very personification of good temper, he will resent to the utmost any insult offered to those under his charge. Then we come to the Donkeys proper, Xenophon Edward, a light steed; and 'Nem. Con.', a charming creature, with a dark coat. (Volo Non Valeo [Maria Gibbons], *We Donkeys in Devon*, 1885)

This is how Maria Gibbons of East Budleigh, Devon, introduced the first of her *We Donkeys* books, under the pseudonym Volo Non Valeo.
Maria was the daughter of John Gibbons of Middlesex. Very little is known about her early life and, although she probably wrote, there is no record of anything published until she was twenty-nine, and a work called *Church or Chapel; One or Both?* appeared under her name. Then came novels, *The Blarney Stone* and *Was It Wise?*, both published in 1872, and *The Old House on the Downs* four years later.
By the 1880s Maria, her mother and Eli, their ancient butler, were all living at Vicarsmead, an historic house in East Budleigh.
When Mrs Gibbons began to have difficulty in getting to church, she had a cart made which could be pulled by a donkey. Later Maria made good use of this idea. In a custom-built cart, drawn by two donkeys and accompanied by her dog Romulus, she took to the roads of Devonshire and wrote books about her travels. '*We Donkeys' in Devon* (1885) was closely followed by '*We Donkeys' on Dartmoor* (1886) and then '*We Donkeys' on the Coast of Devon* (1887).
Maria's books were packed with descriptions of interesting houses, beautiful views, old churches, local characters and the day-to-day problems of her chosen method of travel:

We had some little excitement, however, for we had to cross the railway, and just before we came to it a train passed. Now Xenophon Edward had never seen a train and this awful thing so alarmed him that he turned straight round and point-blank refused to proceed.

Maria Gibbons also lived for a while at Budleigh Salterton and wrote about its history, but both she and her mother were buried in East Budleigh.

75

CHRISTINE HAMLYN

1855–1936
(née Hamlyn-Fane)
Memorial: All Saints'
Church, Clovelly

Clovelly is difficult to write about because it is the old-established beauty queen of England; and knows it. It cannot be left out of any tour because it is unique; an English Amalfi rising sheer from the bay . . . No signs disfigure its bowers: no motor-car may approach within half a mile of its sacrosanct charms, and when an old cottage dies it rises phoenix-like from its ashes exactly as it was, looking at least five hundred

years old, but with 'C.H., 1923', inscribed on it. Those two initials are the secret of Clovelly. (H. V. Morton *In Search of England*, 1927)

The initials C.H. stand for Christine Hamlyn who for fifty-two years lived at Clovelly Court and virtually reigned over Clovelly. In 1884 she inherited the manor from her brother. In 1889 she married Frederick Gosling but her husband assumed the surname of Hamlyn by Royal Licence. Most of Mrs Hamlyn's life was devoted to the preservation, protection and care of the village.

If you visit Clovelly – preferably well out of season – you will see the results of her dedication. Christine Hamlyn restored cottages, and initialled them; she ensured that all cars, coaches, snack bars and souvenir shops remained well out of sight, above the village, and she gave an acre of ground, at the top of the steep cobbled street, as a war memorial to the men of Clovelly who died in the First World War.

Mrs Hamlyn's memorial (apart from the village itself) is in All Saints' Church, at the top of the hill, near Clovelly Court.

Christine Hamlyn's initials on a house in Clovelly

SARAH HEWETT

1838–1903
(née Anning)
Buried: Tiverton
Cemetery

Vather stawl the passen's sheep
A murry Cursmus us'll keep,
Vur us chell 'ave boath vittals an' drink,
But dawnt zay nort about et!
(Sarah Hewett, *The Peasant Speech of Devon*, 1892)

Sarah Hewett wrote what is probably one of the most enjoyable studies of local dialect and local traditions ever compiled.

Born at Cherithorne, Tiverton, she was married there, and also ran a Ladies School at her home. Her first book, *The Peasant Speech of Devon*, was published in 1892 and went into a second edition within

six months. In her introduction she said: 'I have spent a quarter of a century in collecting the words and sentences of which this work is composed' and was clearly delighted that 'Her Majesty the Queen was graciously pleased to accept a copy for the Royal Library at Windsor'.

Sarah Hewett wrote other books, including *West Country Stories* (1896), *Fairies* (1900) and *Nummits and Crummits* (1900). She was buried in Tiverton Cemetery and her work, sadly, has vanished almost without trace.

DOROTHY HOLMAN

1888–1983

Topsham Museum, The
Strand, Topsham

Dorothy Holman was born in Streatham, London, but her roots lay in Devonshire, particularly in Topsham. She was christened in Topsham Methodist Church and visited the town regularly throughout her early life. In 1939, when she was in her fifties, she bought 25 The Strand and lived there for the next forty-three years.

Almost as soon as she moved in, Dorothy started a Youth Club at her home and organized it for twenty years. She also became interested in the idea of a museum there, which would preserve her family history as well as the history of the town. Gradually items of interest were collected – records of the Holmans' boat-building days, drawings, models of ships and other contributions from the people of Topsham. An informal museum began to develop. In 1967 the Royal Albert Memorial Museum, Exeter, took over responsibility and the Topsham Museum was officially opened. Dorothy helped to run it for years and ensured that her home was left to Exeter City Council when she died. The Topsham Museum now flourishes under the care of the Topsham Museum Society.

LADY MARY HOWARD

1596–1671
(née Fitz)

Fitz Memorial: Parish
Church of St Eustachius,
Tavistock

A great deal of confusion surrounds the life of Lady Mary Howard. She is said to have been executed as a witch – quite untrue; to have murdered her husbands – most unlikely; and to haunt the road between Tavistock and Okehampton – very probable!

The facts seem to be that Mary, only child of Sir John Fitz of Fitzford, was only nine when her father committed suicide. She immediately became very valuable as an heiress, and her wardship was bought by the Earl of Northumberland. Three years later she was married off to the Earl's brother, Sir Alan Percy, who thought the high price of the wardship well worth the future profit. Mary was sixteen when he died.

She promptly eloped with the young, handsome but ailing Thomas Darcy. He died within months, and with him went what had probably been Mary's one chance of a love match.

Her third husband, Sir Charles Howard, gave her higher social status – and two daughters – but it was with ever increasing cynicism that she watched this husband raising money from her properties to pay his debts. Eventually Mary put her foot down, broke with her husband, and managed to regain control of half her property. Sir Charles, deeply offended, went abroad and died on his return to England in 1622.

Six years later, having ensured that all her property was under her control, Mary married the dashing Sir Richard Grenville. At first all seemed to be well, but shortly after the birth of their second child Sir Richard tried to prove that his wife's arrangements over her property were invalid.

Mary travelled to London and petitioned for a divorce. She was allowed to live apart from him, but the legal wrangles continued and finally Sir Richard was imprisoned and Mary given her divorce. She returned to Fitzford and called herself Lady Howard for the rest of her life.

After her death, the legend of her 'wickedness' began to circulate. She is said to travel every night from Okehampton Castle to Fitzford Gate, Tavistock, in a coach made of bones, preceded by a phantom dog. One old folk song, supposed to be about her, begins:

My Ladye hath a sable coach,
And horses two and four,
My Ladye hath a gaunt blood-hound,
That runneth on before.
My Ladye's coach hath nodding
  plumes,
The driver hath no head,
My Ladye is an ashen white,
As one that long is dead.

MARY ELFREDA KELLY, OBE

1888–1951

Memorial: Kelly Church, Kelly

The rural theatre of the past had above all, a unity between players and audience; a thing which is certainly equally possible for the village theatre of today. (Mary E. Kelly, *Village Theatre*, 1939)

Mary Kelly's deep interest in village drama probably sprang from the family theatricals that were enjoyed at their home in Kelly, Devon, when she was a girl.

Born at Salcombe, the daughter of a parson, she and her family moved to Kelly in 1900 when her uncle, who was squire there, died. The villagers had a long tradition of performing plays in the old granary and Mary Kelly became involved. Her book *On English Costume* was published in 1925. She wrote plays, pageants and sketches for drama groups, and her study, *Village Theatre*, appeared in 1939.

Eventually the movement became so widespread that Mary handed her responsibilities at Kelly over to a successor. She became Secretary of the Village Drama Society, a new section of the British Drama League, with an office in London. Described as 'a great personality and full of fun' her work for village drama groups in Devon and elsewhere was invaluable.

Mary Kelly was awarded the OBE for her work and there is a memorial to her in Kelly Church. She retired to South Africa to be near her sister, and died at Ikopo, Natal, in 1951.

THE OLD MAIDS OF LEE

c. 1653

The Old Maids' Cottage, Lee

There were three young maids of Lee,
They were fair as fair can be,
And they had lovers three times three,
For they were fair as fair can be,
These three young maids of Lee.
(F. E. Weatherly, 1883)

Lee is a very pretty village by the sea, not far from Ilfracombe, which boasts – amongst other attractions – a picturesque thatched cottage, said to have been built in 1653. It is supposed to have been the home of three 'old maids', who had been too fastidious in their choice of suitors. Fred Weatherly wrote a song about them:

These young maids they cannot find
A lover each to suit her mind.
The plain-spoke lad is far too rough,
The rich young lord is not rich enough.

No one seems to know very much about them, except that they probably lived there in the nineteenth century and that they all suffered a supposedly dreadful fate for being so fussy:

There are three old maids at Lee,
And one is deaf, and one cannot see,
They are old as old can be,
And they all are cross as a gallows tree,
These three old maids of Lee.

ETHEL MANNIN

1900–1984

Lived: Shaldon near Teignmouth

Ethel Mannin was born in London. A prolific writer, she was the author of at least ninety novels, including *Children of the Earth* (1930), *Women also Dream* (1937), *Late Have I Loved Thee* (1948) and *The Curious Adventure of Major Fosdick* (1972).

Married twice, to J. A. Porteous in 1920 and to Reginald Reynolds in 1938, she had one daughter. She joined the Independent Labour Party in 1932 but resigned about seven years later.

In 1974 Ethel Mannin bought a bungalow near Teignmouth, Devon, and lived there for the rest of her life. Her last autobiographical work, *Sunset Over Dartmoor*, was written there and published in 1977:

You cannot be bored by the ebb and flow of tides, the wheeling of gulls, the bobbing of boats and buoys, the massing of clouds on hills, the changing light and shade on water.

78

SARAH CATHERINE MARTIN

1768–1826

Old Mother Hubbard's Cottage, Yealmpton

Old Mother Hubbard
Went to the cupboard
To fetch her poor dog a bone.

One of the best-known English nursery rhymes was written by Sarah Martin while she was staying at Kitley Court, near Yealmpton, in 1804. The fifteen verses, accompanied by Sarah's delightful illustrations and published in 1805, were an instant success, selling over ten thousand copies within a few months.

There has been much scholarly discussion as to whether Sarah's 'Old Mother Hubbard' was entirely original, or whether she was inspired by a much older version of the same subject, but no one seems to have reached any positive conclusion.

She is said to have written it when her host, irritated by her incessant chatter, suggested that she should go away and write one of her 'stupid little rhymes':

She took a clean dish
To get him some tripe,
But when she came back
He was smoking a pipe.

Sarah, extremely pretty and vivacious, did not marry but was once romantically involved with royalty:

Her father was naval Commissioner of Portsmouth, and while stationed there, Prince William Henry (later King William IV) arrived in H.M.S. Hebe, on which he was then serving as a Lieutenant. He became not only a frequent visitor, but rather an inmate of the Commissioner's house, with the result that he fell violently in love with, and offered his hand and heart in marriage, to Miss Sarah. (*The Essex Review*, 1917)

The affair was considered to be quite unsuitable and Sarah was packed off to her aunt's home in London. Prince William was despatched to the West Indies, but it all seems to have been handled with great tact and no one was broken-hearted:

The dame made a curtsey
The dog made a bow;
The dame said, Your servant
The dog said, Bow-wow.

FRANCES, VISCOUNTESS NELSON, DUCHESS OF BRONTË

1758–1831
(née Frances Herbert Woolward)

Buried: St Margaret and St Andrew's Churchyard, Littleham
Monument: inside the church

Let me beg, nay intreat you, to believe no wife ever felt greater affection for her husband than I do. And to the best of my knowledge I have invariably done everything you desired. If I have omitted any thing I am sorry for it.

Poor Frances! Her husband, Vice-Admiral Horatio Lord Nelson, has always been venerated as the ideal British hero. The despair and loneliness of his wife over her broken marriage has inevitably been played down.

Emma Hamilton, Nelson's mistress, has always managed to steal the limelight.

In March 1787, on the Island of Nevis, Captain Nelson married an attractive young widow, with a seven-year-old son by her first marriage. Frances Nisbet had grey eyes, fine features and an exquisite complexion. She spoke French fluently, was an expert needlewoman and was also a little nervous and highly strung.

For three years their marriage

SACRED TO THE MEMORY OF
FRANCES HERBERT,
VISCOUNTESS NELSON DUCHESS OF BRONTI,
WIDOW OF THE LATE ADMIRAL LORD VISCOUNT NELSON

seemed to be reasonably happy but, on 24 November 1800, they appeared for the last time together in public. The following year they met for the last time.

Frances took care of her father-in-law, worried about money, retired to Devon and eventually died there. As consolation, she had grandchildren by the son of her first marriage. They, at least, must have helped to heal her wounded pride and ease the memory of the husband who once wrote to her:

> For most sincerely do I love you . . . Indeed, my charming Fanny, did I possess a million, my greatest pride and pleasure would be to share it with you; and as to living in a cottage with you, I should esteem it superior to living in a palace with any other I have yet met with.

ELEANOR ANNE ORMEROD

1828–1901
Lived: Torquay

Eleanor Ormerod was born at Sedbury, West Gloucestershire. A lively mischievous little girl, she was educated at home, allowed free use of her father's library, and soon began to show signs of an acute intellect and strong powers of observation. She helped one of her brothers with his botanical work and soon became an expert at preparing specimens, but the real milestone in her life was the moment she acquired a copy of Stephens's *Manual of British Beetles*. From then on, she devoted her life to the study of insects. She became an economic entomologist, the author of many books on the subject and, eventually, the first woman Honorary Graduate of the University of Edinburgh (1900).

On the death of their father, Eleanor and her sister Georgiana moved to Devon, and lived at Torquay for several years. Another sister, Mary, settled in Exeter, and their brother, George, in Teignmouth.

EULALIA (OR ELIZABETH) PAGE

d. 1591
(née Glanville)
Tried: Barnstaple

In March 1591, four prisoners were tried at Barnstaple in Devon for the murder of an elderly goldsmith named Page, all of Plymouth. They were all found guilty and hanged. One of them was Eulalia Page, the goldsmith's young wife.

This sensational event captured the imagination of the public and was immediately celebrated in popular ballads of the time. It was also turned into a play.

Eulalia Glanville, the daughter of a Tavistock merchant, fell desperately in love with a young man called George Stanwich, also of Tavistock. Stanwich was considered to be unsuitable by her family, and Eulalia was forbidden to marry him. Taking advantage of this situation, Page, a goldsmith who lived in Plymouth, made a tempting financial offer and Eulalia – who had not heard from her lover and was under considerable family pressure – married him, and moved to Plymouth. Very soon after this Stanwich turned up and, when Eulalia accused him of not having written to her, they realized that his letters had been intercepted.

No one knows exactly what happened next. One night it seems a neighbour of the Pages, disturbed by an unusual noise, got out of bed and went to her window. She saw the figure of a young man and thought she heard him say: 'For God's sake stay your hand'. A woman's voice replied: 'It is too late; the deed is done!' The next morning it was announced that Page had died suddenly and he was rather hurriedly buried. However, after the neighbour's report to the authorities, his body was disinterred and it was discovered that he had been strangled.

Eulalia, George Stanwich, and two others were arrested and condemned to death.

JANE PARMINTER
1750?–1811

MARY PARMINTER
1766–1849
Lived: 'A La Ronde', near Exmouth

An extraordinary and fantastical house called 'A La Ronde' lies off Summer Lane, just north of Exmouth. In 1985 it celebrated its fiftieth year open to the public. Check opening times before you visit – but visit you must.

A La Ronde was completed in 1798, built to the specifications of two cousins, Jane and Mary Parminter, inspired by the Basilica of San Vitale at Ravenna, Italy, which they had visited while touring Europe. When the house was finished, Jane and Mary set to work and decorated it. They decorated with feathers, they decorated with shells, they made

pictures from sand and seaweed, and they filled every available space with collections and curiosities, from a miniature bookcase complete with tiny books to a rare 'silhouette' by Torond. The whole thing is fascinating and one visit is barely sufficient.

The house itself almost defies description. It is not *ronde* but sixteen-sided, with rooms on all floors, radiating from a central octagonal hall, lit from above by a lantern. Not far away are a chapel and almshouses, also founded by the two cousins and named Point in View. Jane and Mary are buried in the chapel beneath the organ.

MRS PARTINGTON

fl. 1824
Lived: Chit Rock, Sidmouth

As for the possibility of the House of Lords preventing ere long a reform of Parliament, I hold it to be the most absurd notion that ever entered into human imagination. I do not mean to be disrespectful, but the attempt of the Lords to stop the progress of reform, reminds me very forcibly of the great storm at Sidmouth, and of the conduct of the excellent Mrs Partington on that occasion. (Sydney Smith, in a speech at Taunton, *c.* 1831)

Few of us would expect to feature as an analogy in a political speech, but Mrs Partington *had* made herself rather conspicuous. She lived in a small cottage at Chit Rock, Sidmouth, very much exposed to the elements at the best of times. In 1824, a terrible gale blew up and huge waves were hurled against the town:

Mrs Partington . . . saw her kitchen floor invaded by the sea and resented the intrusion. Rolling up her sleeves, she secured her petticoats . . . picked up her mop, and set to work to sweep the Atlantic out. She got one corner dry, but the Atlantic did not know when it was beaten and poured in ruthlessly . . . fate was on the side of the big battalions, and Mrs Partington, faint but pursuing, was well and truly beaten by the ocean. (Arthur Mee, *Devon*, 1938)

Sydney Smith, poet, essayist and wit, used the story to illustrate the impossibility of preventing political reform. His well-known and highly successful speech ended with these words:

She was excellent with a slop or a puddle, but she should not have meddled with a tempest. Gentlemen, be at your ease. Be quiet and steady. You will beat Mrs Partington.

ANN (NANCY) PERRIAM

1767?–1865
Lived: Tower Street, Exmouth

Reference to the exploits of Ann Perriam of Exmouth, ancestor of the present Chairman of Exmouth Council . . . was made by Mr W.J. Perriam . . . proposing a toast to the Royal Navy at the dinner given in honour of the Officers of H.M.S. Exmouth on Saturday night. (The *Western Morning News*, June 1938)

'Nancy' Perriam has never been forgotten in Exmouth – but then it is not every town that can boast of a woman who not only served in the Navy during some of the most

important battles in British history, but at one time under Admiral Lord Nelson himself.

Nancy was in her twenties when she was first allowed to accompany her sailor husband on board the warships *Crescent* and *Orion* – her brother also served on the same ships. She became what was known as a 'powder monkey', stationed in the magazine with the gunners, and preparing flannel cartridge cases for the big guns. *The Gentleman's Magazine* of 1865 listed the battles in which she had taken part: L'Orient, under Admiral Lord Bridport (1795); off Cape St Vincent, under Admiral Sir John Jervis (1797), and the Battle of the Nile, under Admiral Lord Nelson (1798). She was also present during several lesser naval occasions.

When she returned home Nancy Perriam lived in Tower Street, Exmouth, and was much admired and greatly respected. She eventually became a female Naval pensioner, receiving ten pounds a year from the Government until her death in 1865.

Portrait of Nancy Perriam

VIOLET PINWILL

1874–1957
Pulpit, St Peter's Church,
Stoke Fleming

She was by far the most skilled wood-carver in the West Country. She was a fine teacher and a marvellous technician. . . . Her work was always in the Gothic manner and fitted beautifully with the old work in churches. It was easily recognisable by its perfection of workmanship. (Mr Lewis Duckett, Plymouth College of Art, 1957)

Violet Pinwill was a wood carver, who specialized in church wood restoration work. A few days before her death she was putting the finishing touches to a five-foot figure of St Peter for St Peter's Church in Blackburn, Lancashire, and had current work in progress for no less than five counties in England. At least ninety churches, most of them in Cornwall and Devon, have examples of her work.

With such an amazing output one can only list a few examples, such as the exquisite carving on the pulpit at St Peter's Church, Stoke Fleming, and the stand for the Book of Remembrance, as well as the saints on the Canon's stalls, in Truro Cathedral. Most of the interior of St Gabriel's church at Postbridge, on Dartmoor, is Violet Pinwill's work. She also carved an unusual seat-end in the church of St Martin-by-Looe, as a memorial to a young man drowned in a remote valley of the Himalayas.

One of the seven daughters of the Reverend Edmund Pinwill and his wife, Violet was born in Moulton, Lancashire. When she

was six, the family moved to Ermington in Devon, where her father was to remain as vicar for the next forty-four years.

During his tenure, money became available for the much needed restoration of the church, and a team of experts arrived to carry out the work. Mrs Pinwill suggested that three of her daughters should have lessons in wood-carving in the evenings, and so the apprenticeship began. The sisters eventually went into business under the name of Rashleigh Pinwill & Co., and in 1900 they moved to premises in Plymouth. Violet, now very much in charge, employed six men. This was later to increase to twenty-nine.

Violet also taught at Plymouth Technical College for many years. Her family have described her as shy of publicity but extremely energetic and hard-working:

> She did everything herself and thought nothing of setting out at dawn in a 'workman's' train for the remotest part of the country, like Sennen Church at Land's End, to consult vicars and churchwardens about their requirements.

In 1942 she donated a collection of carved woodwork, saved from West Country churches where she had worked, to the City Museum and Art Gallery, Plymouth. Violet Pinwill died in Plymouth but was buried in Ermington churchyard.

Opposite: **The pulpit carved by Violet Pinwill in St Peter's Church, Stoke Fleming**

85

Memorial to Agnes Prest at the junction of Denmark and Barnfield Roads, Exeter

AGNES PREST

c. 1503–1557

Memorial: Junction of
Denmark and Barnfield
Roads, Exeter

In the reign of Bloody Mary, the wife
of one Prest was brought before
[Bishop] Turbeville for denying the
real presence in the mass. She was
condemned to be burnt, which
horrible sentence was carried out at
Southernhay, 15th August, 1557.
This deed should never be forgotten
by the people of this city. (*The
Chronicles of Exeter*, 1668)

The people of Exeter did not
forget. In 1909 a memorial was
erected there, at the junction of
Denmark and Barnfield Roads, 'in
grateful remembrance' of two

Protestant martyrs, Thomas Benet
and Agnes Prest.

Agnes, aged fifty-four and a wife
and mother, was hunted down,
indicted at Launceston (Cornwall),
and thrown into prison. Among
other heresies she was accused of
saying that 'No Christian doth eat
the Body of Christ carnally but
spiritually'. Although under
considerable pressure, she refused
to recant and died in front of
gaping crowds outside the city
walls of Exeter.

FRANCES REYNOLDS

1729–1807

Born: Plympton
St Maurice

Joshua Reynolds – artist, first
President of the Royal Academy,
knighted in 1769 – was born at
Plympton St Maurice in 1723. Six
years later a sister arrived, and was
christened Frances. Their father
was headmaster of the Grammar
School. When he was seventeen
Joshua was apprenticed to the
painter, Hudson, in London and
later studied in Italy. Frances
stayed at home and painted
miniatures.

After their father's death the
family moved to Plymouth Dock
(now Devonport) and later to a
house in London. Frances, aged
about twenty-four, became her

brother's housekeeper. Although
kept very busy running the house
and entertaining visitors, she
continued to try to teach herself to
paint, getting little encouragement
from Joshua:

> She copied her brother's pictures
> assiduously in water-colours but he
> never gave her the slightest
> instruction, and hated to see her at
> work. (Ellen Clayton, 1876)

Sir Joshua Reynolds became one
of the most important figures in the
history of British Art. His sister left
behind some interesting portraits
of friends and acquaintances,
including Hannah More (q.v.).

ELIZABETH POSTHUMA SIMCOE

1766–1850
(née Gwillim)

Buried: Wolford Chapel
near Honiton

Elizabeth Gwillim of Hereford
married Lieutenant-Colonel John
Graves Simcoe in 1782. They lived
for a short while in Exeter, Devon,
but in 1784 bought the 5,000 acre
Wolford Estate, near Honiton, and
four years later moved into their
new home, Wolford Lodge. They
took with them their five
daughters.

John Graves Simcoe was elected
Member of Parliament for St
Mawes and then chosen as the first
Lieutenant-Governor of the new
Province of Upper Canada.

When Elizabeth left for Canada
in 1791, she took with her one of
her daughters, Sophie, and her
six-month-old baby son. They

arrived in Quebec on 11
November and remained in
Canada until 1796. Elizabeth rode,
walked, sketched and kept a diary
throughout her stay there:

> Wed. 25th – A clear, cold day; made
> little way – a head wind. I saw the
> spray of the Falls of Niagara rising
> like a cloud. It is 40 miles distant . . .
> We walked to the spot intended for
> the site of the town [later to be
> Toronto]. Mr Aitkin's canoe was
> there; we went into it, and himself
> and his man paddled . . . To see a
> birch canoe managed with that
> inexpressible care and composure,
> which is the characteristic of an
> Indian, is the prettiest sight
> imaginable. A man usually paddles at
> one end of it and a woman at the

other; but in smooth water little exertion is wanting, and they sit quietly as if to take the air. The canoe appears to move as if by clockwork.

Elizabeth gave birth to another daughter. Although she must have missed the children she had left in Devon, she was sorry to leave Canada. When she arrived back in England almost her last words in the diary speak of the 'damp, raw and unpleasant' weather and the fields, which looked 'so cold . . . so cheerless, so uncomfortable from the want of our bright Canadian sun'. Nevertheless, Elizabeth Simcoe settled back into life at Wolford Lodge with few complaints and after her husband's death founded a new church, Holy Trinity, on the site of Dunkeswell Abbey. She is buried at Wolford Chapel, between Dunkeswell and Honiton.

Portrait of Mrs Simcoe

THE SIMCOE SISTERS

fl. nineteenth century

Plate and corbels:
St Nicholas, Dunkeswell

The church of St Nicholas at Dunkeswell, Devon, was rebuilt between 1865 and 1868. To the right of the door as you enter is a brass plate, commemorating 'the departed sisters of Wolford Lodge' – the six surviving daughters of Mrs Elizabeth Simcoe (q.v.) and John Graves Simcoe, the first Governor of Upper Canada.

There are six delightful angel corbels in the church. Each one is a portrait of one of the sisters, and each one has her initials carved below her face: Eliza, Charlotte, Henrietta Maria, Caroline, Sophia Jemima and Katharine. All of them

were well-known for their kindness and charitable works in the district. Their lives, however, were ruled with a rod of iron. Although they were all attractive, and very marriageable, their mother:

> sternly discouraged all the Misses Simcoe's suitors and refused in their names those eligible young men who had the temerity to ask her for her daughters' hands. They all died spinsters except one, who dared to marry only after her mother's death. (A. Mackenzie-Grieve, *The Great Accomplishment*, 1953)

Opposite: Angel corbel of one of the Simcoe sisters – Sophia Jemima – in St Nicholas, Durkeswell

MARIANA STARKE

1762?–1838
Lived: 11 The Beacon, Exmouth

There were Roberts from
   Courtlands, from Nutwell the
   Mills;
From Bicton Place Mr and the Miss
   Hills;
Miss Gilbert was there, and to join
   the gay set,
And add harmony, too, there was
   Mrs Divett,
And her daughter; and last, but not
   least worthy remark,
The famed, and the gifted, and the
   talented Starke.
   (*Exmouth Journal*, 1933)

Mariana Starke, who lived at 11 The Beacon, Exmouth, was a most unusual woman. She wrote one of the earliest travel guides as we know them today – preceding not only Murray's Guides, but also the famous Baedeker.

Her father was Governor of Fort St George in Madras and Mariana spent her childhood in India. As a young woman in England, she began to write plays, but soon moved to Italy where she spent seven years nursing a consumptive relative. She was nearly forty when her book *Letters from Italy, 1792–1798* was published, in two volumes. Based on her considerable experience of travelling around and living on the Continent, it was a lively, sensible and humorous guide, filled with information on the best routes to take, sites to see, and where to shop.

By 1811, Mariana was living in Exmouth with her mother. She visited Italy again and then published *Travels on the Continent* (1820). In Exmouth she took an interest in local affairs and helped to organize the more spectacular celebrations of the town. As she grew older, her eccentricities provoked a certain amount of affectionate amusement there:

In her days the portion of the Strand Enclosure between what is now Lloyds Bank, on the west side, and Ball and Co's establishment on the eastern, was a public garden . . . and Miss Starke might often be seen in a man's hat, with spade and rake on her shoulder, coming down the hill to work in the garden. In polite society she was known as the Queen of Sorrento, in ruder circles as Jack Starke. (*Exmouth Journal*, 1933)

In her seventies, Mariana Starke set off for another visit to Italy. She died in Milan, on her way home, in 1838.

MARY THOMAS

fl. 1816
St Andrew's Church, Cullompton

Memorial by Mary Thomas in St Andrew's Church, Cullompton

Hardly anything at all is known about Mary Thomas except that she came from Exmouth and that, at some point in her life, she followed the unusual career of a monumental mason.

Unfortunately, her tablet to Charles Fanshawe in the Temple Church, London, sculpted in 1814 was destroyed during the Second World War. However, her signed memorial to the Heathfield family can still be seen on a wall in the superb old church of St Andrew's, Cullompton, Devon.

FLORA THOMPSON

**1876–1947
(née Timms)
Buried: Longcross
Cemetery, Dartmouth**

Flora Thompson needs no introduction to those who have read *Lark Rise to Candleford* (her three books, *Lark Rise*, *Over to Candleford* and *Candleford Green* were published as a trilogy in 1945). The daughter of a poor stonemason, Flora was born in Juniper Hill, Oxfordshire. By the time she was fourteen she had left school and had begun work in the Post Office at Fringford. When she was nearly twenty, she moved to Hampshire and became post office assistant in the village of Grayshott.

When she was twenty-four, Flora married John Thompson, a post office clerk from Aldershot, and moved to Bournemouth, where she gave birth to a daughter and then a son. Her early attempts to write seem to have been discouraged by her husband and his family, but she persevered, with poetry, short stories and magazine articles.

In 1916 the Thompsons moved to Hampshire where Flora's third child was born, and then to Dartmouth in Devon. It was here that Flora began to write about her childhood and, in 1939, when she was sixty-three, *Lark Rise* was published. Encouraged by her publishers, she produced *Over to Candleford* (1941) and then *Candleford Green*. Sadly, her success came too late to afford her any real pleasure: 'Twenty years ago I should have been beside myself with joy, but I am now too old to care much for the bubble reputation.'

Living in a cottage at Brixham, where she and her husband had retired, she managed to finish *Still Glides the Stream* just before her death.

Flora Thompson was buried in Longcross Cemetery, Dartmouth, in Devon.

CHARLOTTE ELIZABETH TREADWIN

**1821–1890
Buried: Higher
Cemetery, Exeter**

WHITE LACE NOT TO BE DYED BLACK
No white lace should ever be dyed black, and it is perfectly useless when done, for when it is remembered that all black lace is made of *silk* and white lace of *thread*, the reason for never attempting to dye it will be at once perceived. (Mrs Treadwin, *Antique Point, Honiton Lace*, 1873)

Superb lace was produced in Devon for centuries, and many women there became experts in this beautiful craft. Charlotte Treadwin was one of the most successful and influential figures in the late nineteenth century.

Born near Dulverton, Somerset, Charlotte was apprenticed to a dressmaker of North Molton in Devon. Some time before 1841 – probably after her marriage – she opened a lace shop in the Cathedral Close at Exeter, and received the Royal Warrant in 1848.

Her work was shown at various exhibitions, including the Great Exhibition of London in 1851, and four years later she was awarded a first-class medal in Paris.

Mrs Treadwin also ran a

Wedding Veil made by Mrs Treadwin at All Hallows Museum, Honiton workshop at her house, where she employed lace-workers on major commissions. She had designs made for her at the Government School of Design, Somerset House, London, and in 1873 published *Antique Point, Honiton Lace*. Her interest in lace-making was historical as well as practical – in 1869 Mrs Palliser, in her *History of Lace*, noted that 'Mrs Treadwin, of Exeter, found an old lace-worker using a lace "turn" fo winding sticks, having the date 1678 rudely carved on the foot, showing how the trade was continued in the same families from generation to generation.'

Mrs Treadwin died aged sixty-nine and was buried in the Higher Cemetery at Exeter.

IRENE VANBRUGH

1872–1949
(Mrs Boucicault)
(née Barnes)

VIOLET VANBRUGH

1867–1942
(Mrs Bourchier)
(née Barnes)
Lived: Heavitree
Vicarage, Exeter

I want you to try to see with me the low, two-storeyed vicarage at Heavitree, near Exeter, with its ground-floor windows opening on to a simple but beautiful garden. I should like you to stand at the night nursery window with me and see, as I do now, the smooth green lawn stretching down from a wide gravel walk. There is a large walnut tree on the left from which a swing hangs.
(Irene Vanbrugh, *To Tell My Story*, 1948)

Irene and Violet were the daughters of the Reverend Reginald Barnes, vicar of Heavitree and Prebendary of Exeter Cathedral. They both became well-known actresses and spent all their lives working in, an for, the British theatre. Violet married Arthur Bourchier, Irene, Dion Boucicault. In 1941 Irene Vanbrugh was created DBE for he services to the stage.

The stage-name of 'Vanbrugh', which they both adopted, was suggested to Violet as a fashionable conceit, by the actress Ellen Terry.

AGNES ELIZABETH WESTON

1840–1918
Buried: Weston Mill
Cemetery, Devonport

To provide a home for Jack and to run it for him is not all easy sailing, and I do not advise any one who wants to have 'a quiet time of it' to run a Sailors' Rest nowadays. I sometimes get blamed for things for which I am not responsible but I have many brave and bold champions on the lower deck who stand up vigorously for me. (Agnes Weston, *My Life Among the Blue-Jackets*, 1909)

Agnes Weston – known as 'Aggie' – and her friend, Sophie Wintz, were co-founders of 'Sailors' Rests', or Temperance Hotels for sailors, in Devonport and Portsmouth (Hants).

An amazingly energetic woman, Aggie's deep belief in Christianity, her commitment to the Temperance movement and her sincere affection for the ordinary British sailor led her to dedicate almost forty years of her life to him. Her strongest points were her sense of humour and the fact that she understood and sympathized with the men who, returning from a long, unnatural life at sea, were unable to resist the temptations awaiting them on shore. She also realized the devastating effect this might have on their wives and children.

Her monthly 'letter' first distributed to ships' companies in 1871, eventually achieved a circulation of sixty thousand and in 1874 she was asked to provide a temperance house near the dockyard gates at Devonport. Thi was opened two years later. In 1881 Aggie and Sophie Wintz opened a second 'Sailors' Rest' at Portsmouth in Hampshire.

Aggie Weston wrote her memoirs, *My Life Among the Blue-Jackets*, published in 1909, and was created DBE in 1918. She died the same year and was buried in Weston Mill Cemetery, Devonport, one of very few women to be given a funeral with full Naval honours.

Agnes Weston's grave at Weston Mill Cemetery, Devonport

MRS HENRY PENNELL WHITCOMBE

d. 1887
(née Joce)
Born: Kerscott, near
Swimbridge

Miss Joce was born at Kerscott, Swimbridge. In 1862 she married Henry Pennell Whitcombe. Her book, *Bygone Days in Devonshire and Cornwall with notes of existing Superstitions and Customs* was published in 1874 and was packed with ancient and neglected legends. It also described charming, if rather vague, customs:

> The children in the southern division of the county carry about, on May 29, little dolls, prettily dressed, and laid in white boxes – these they call 'May babies'. The origin of this is supposed to be connected in some way with Charles II.

Mrs Pennell Whitcombe often discovered superstitions that were clearly based on a sincere belief –

such as placing a prayer-book under a baby's pillow, to prevent lurking 'piskies' from stealing the baby. But there were also moments when she was surely the victim of her informant's sense of humour:

> Many of the country-folk will assure you that, on seeing the first new moon in the year, if you take a stocking off one foot, and run across a field, you will then find a hair between the great toe and the next, which will be the colour of your lover's.

Unfortunately, Mrs Whitcombe did not pursue her imaginative research but moved to London and in 1884 her *Cheap Choice Cooking for Small Families* was published. She died in London three years later.

DORSET

There is a small book called *The Story of Shaftesbury Abbey*, based on a talk by Phyllis Carter. She mentions, briefly and modestly, that she and a friend, Laura Sydenham, bought the site of the abbey ruins in 1951. They 'felt it was a challenge to get it on to its feet again . . . Our enthusiasm and love of Dorset has made the task well worth while.'

The history of the abbey is fascinating and it is well and thoroughly recorded in Laura Sydenham's *Shaftesbury and its Abbey* (1959). From AD 888, when the Benedictine abbey for women was consecrated, to 1539, when the abbey was surrendered to the Crown and Elizabeth Zouch, the last abbess, left with her nuns, it was run by, and for, women. Thirty-three abbesses are recorded, among them the mysterious 'J' in 1216. One of the most interesting in the twelfth century, was the Abbess Marie – or 'Marie de France', as she called herself. The daughter of Geoffrey of Anjou, she

was a sophisticated and intellectual woman. Laura Sydenham says of her:

> Accustomed to court life in an age of romanticism and exaggerated chivalry, when most women were nonentities, she was a cultured scholar, a linguist and writer. Of her famous lays she says that she 'collected and translated them in honour of a noble king', assumed to be her half-brother Henry.

Later, in 1312, Elizabeth, the wife of Robert Bruce, was brought to the abbey with her stepdaughter Marjorie. They stayed there as prisoners but two years later left for a nunnery at Barking. Two hundred years after this, Catherine of Aragon visited the abbey. She was on her way to marry Henry VII's son, Arthur. No one knew then that she would become the first wife of Henry VIII – nor that, within forty years, the Abbey would be signed away and all the nuns pensioned off. The life of the abbey was almost over.

VALENTINE
ACKLAND
1906–1969
buried: St Nicholas'
Churchyard, Chaldon
Herring (East Chaldon)

Valentine Ackland was a poet, and the close friend of Sylvia Townsend Warner (q.v.). The two women met in Dorset and eventually settled there, near Maiden Newton. In 1934 they published a collection of their poetry, *Whether a Dove or Seagull*. Valentine Ackland drew much of her imagery from the beautiful countryside of Dorset. Her verse has a fine emotional intensity:

'Blossom, my darling, Blossom, be a rose –'
Blossom into a rose as you are bidden,
Woman – Remain at that and be unchidden,
Beloved and love – given, complete –
Or straggle into a tree and have the world at your feet.

She was buried in the churchyard of St Nicholas, Chaldon Herring (East Chaldon).

MARY ANNING

1799–1847

Memorial: Lyme Parish
Church Window
Buried: Lyme Parish
Churchyard

I cannot close this notice of our losses by death without adverting to that of one, who though not placed among even the easier classes of society, but who had to earn her daily bread by her labour, yet contributed by her talents and untiring researches in no small degree to our knowledge of the great Enalio-Saurians, and other forms of organic life entombed in the vicinity of Lyme Regis. (Sir Henry De La Beche, Anniversary Address to the Geological Society, 1848)

Due to its particular geological situation Lyme Regis has been a paradise to geologists, palaeontologists and collectors of fossils for more than two hundred years. Today, shops there not only sell a variety of fossils, but sometimes display the latest exciting discovery in their windows. Fossil hunters are easily identified among the crowds of holidaymakers by their geologist's hammers, and a certain air of serious, yet happy dedication.

Some of the greatest finds at Lyme came during the early part of the nineteenth century, and one of those involved was Mary Anning.

Mary was born in Lyme Regis, the daughter of a cabinet maker. Both her parents collected fossils and Mary and her brother, Joseph, learnt the art from an early age. Selling their finds was a small but necessary supplement to the family income, a necessity that became urgent when their father died in 1810. Mary may have been with her brother when he discovered the first complete ichthyosaurus in 1811.

Gradually, encouraged by the three Philpot sisters (q.v.), Mary began to study the whole subject in greater depth. In 1824 she found the first complete plesiosaurus and in 1828 a pterosaur (flying reptile) dimorphodon. She often worked with eminent palaeontologists, notably Henry De La Beche, who became President of the Geological Society, and William Buckland, and they in turn helped to make her name known. She sold some of her finds to collectors, such as the Duke of Buckingham and the King of Saxony.

Mary Anning died in 1847 aged forty-eight. She was buried in the churchyard of the parish church at Lyme. Inside the church there is a memorial window to her, which was paid for by the Geological Society and the vicar. Many of the fossils she found are in the Natural History Museum in London.

MARY, LADY BANKES

d. 1661
(née Hawtrey)
Lived: Corfe Castle

Mary was the only daughter of Ralph Hawtrey of Ruislip. She married Sir John Bankes, Attorney-General and later Chief Justice of Common Pleas, in the reign of Charles I. Altogether, Lady Bankes gave birth to thirteen children and ten of them survived.

From 1635 her home was Corfe Castle in Dorset, and everything in Lady Bankes's life pales into insignificance beside her defence of this castle against Parliamentary forces.

Today Corfe Castle stands, a truly romantic ruin, on its mound above the little town. In 1646 the House of Commons voted to demolish the castle so that it would never again cause them any problems.

Sir John Bankes and his family were loyal to the King and when the Civil War began and Charles I moved the court to Oxford, Sir John accompanied him, leaving his family in Dorset. Lady Bankes had a shrewd idea of what might happen next – Parliament could hardly leave her husband's property unchallenged. In 1643 she prepared for the inevitable siege:

> A proclamation was made at Wareham that no beef, beer, or other provisions should be sold to Lady Bankes or for her use. No messengers were permitted to pass into or out of the castle. (Viola Bankes, *A Dorset Heritage*, 1953)

Eventually surrounded by Parliamentary troops, Lady Bankes, with a tiny garrison of servants and helpers, held out for thirteen weeks. When further Royalist military help arrived the siege was lifted and there was a temporary respite.

In December 1644 Sir John Bankes died at Oxford and six months later Corfe Castle was under siege once more. It was only through treachery that the defence of the castle was undermined in the spring of 1646.

Mary, Lady Bankes was forced to leave. She was allowed to keep the keys and seals of the castle in recognition of her bravery, but had to leave everything she owned behind. Her last years were spent at Damory Court, Blandford in Dorset, but she was buried at Ruislip, Middlesex.

Corfe Castle

LUCY EMILY BAXTER (LEADER SCOTT)

1837–1902
(née Barnes)
Born: Dorchester

By the regretted death of Mrs Baxter, better known outside Italy by her 'nom de guerre' of Leader Scott, a notable figure disappears from the Literary Society of Florence . . . Mrs Baxter was a persona grata in literary and artistic Italian circles, always generously ready to encourage and honour intellectual ability in a woman; and the Academia delle Belle Arti some years ago elected her an honorary member of their Society in recognition of her work in interpreting certain aspects of Italian art. (*The Athenaeum*, November 1902)

Lucy Baxter died in the Villa Bianca, on the outskirts of Florence, Italy. She was born at Dorchester, Dorset, the third daughter of William Barnes, the poet, schoolmaster and clergyman who became known as 'the Dorsetshire Poet'. Lucy began writing herself at the age of

seventeen. Longing to visit Italy, she saved every penny she made from short stories and magazine articles, until she had enough money to realize her dream.

In 1867 she met, and married, Samuel Baxter, whose family had been in Italy for many years, and Lucy lived in her adopted country for the rest of her life. She had four children but continued to write, concentrating on her main interests, Italian art and architecture. She wrote *Ghiberti and Donatello, etc.* (1882), *The Renaissance of Art in Italy* (1883), *Tuscan Studies and Sketches* (1887) and *Echoes of Old Florence* (1894). Her main work, *The Cathedral Builders*, a study of the work of the Comacine masons, was published in 1899.

ELIZABETH MARTHA BROWN

d. 1856
Executed: Dorchester
Gaol

It is generally accepted that the hanging of Martha Brown at Dorchester in 1856 provided the emotional inspiration for Thomas Hardy's novel, *Tess of the D'Urbervilles* (1891). Hardy, aged sixteen, joined the crowd of several thousand outside Dorchester Gaol on the morning of the execution and climbed a tree so that he could see better. It was raining and, when the white hood was placed over Martha Brown's head, the material clung to her features. The executioner also tied her dress round her ankles. Thomas Hardy never forgot the incident and was to mention it several times in his old age. He once wrote 'what a fine figure she showed against the sky as she hung in the misty rain, and how the tight black silk gown set off her shape as she wheeled half round and back'.

Martha Brown was hanged for killing her husband, John, who was a carter. They lived in the village of Birdsmoor Gate in West Dorset and it is said that Martha,

although still a beautiful woman, was considerably older than her husband. John was having an affair with a young woman and, one day, Martha saw them together. When her husband came home that night she accused him of being unfaithful and a violent quarrel flared up. John hit her with his whip and Martha, picking up a hatchet, retaliated and killed him.

There was much local and public sympathy for Martha but, unfortunately she persisted in trying to conceal her crime, saying that her husband had been kicked by a horse. She eventually admitted everything and explained the circumstances and the extreme provocation that had led to her action, but it was too late. A reprieve was refused.

When it came to her execution, Martha Brown was described as being perfectly calm. She shook hands with prison officials and showed no apparent fear as she walked to the scaffold.

MARY BUTTS

1890–1937

Born: Salterns, Poole
Buried: Sennen
Churchyard, Sennen,
Cornwall

England is very much a countryman's country: not too large, not too up and down, delicately various, inequable within a pleasant mean. Private, bird-haunted . . . exacting and giving what breeds as good a man as has ever been bred on earth. And on this land has been written the history of that man . . . his beautiful and terrible works, his conquests of nature and his compromises with her . . . until today, after the last hundred years, his denial of her has spread like a nest of sores. (Mary Butts, *A Warning to Hikers*, 1932)

Mary Butts was born at Salterns, on the edge of Poole Harbour in Dorset. She loved the countryside with passion and its gradual destruction, by those she called the 'new barbarians', caused her great anguish.

Mary was educated at St Leonards, the well-known girls' school in St Andrews, Fife, Scotland. She married the writer and publisher John Rodker, by whom she had a daughter, but left him and went to live in Paris

where, in 1928, she published *Imaginary Letters*, illustrated by Jean Cocteau. She once described her life in Paris as 'gay and rather mad' and after an unhappy love affair, she returned to England, ill and exhausted. She eventually settled in Cornwall with her second husband, Gabriel Aitken.

Among her novels, short stories and essays, Mary's *Ashe of Rings* was published in 1925, *Death of Felicity Taverner* in 1932 and *The Macedonian*, a study of Alexander the Great, in 1933. She died aged only forty-six and was buried at Sennen in Cornwall. Her autobiography, *The Crystal Cabinet*, covering the first part of her life, was published posthumously:

I shall never see it again. Except from a long way off. From Purbeck, from the top of Nine Barrow Down, it is still possible to stand, and see, on a clear day, the maggot-knot of dwellings that was once my home.

Portrait of Mary Butts

ALICE MILDRED CABLE

1878–1952
Lived: Willow Cottage,
Stour Row, near
Shaftesbury

We had all lived for many years in the East, and were used to the leisurely pace of Oriental life. We had followed many of the trunk roads of China and were familiar with the varied life of the Chinese people. We knew their language, were at home with their customs and habits, and in matters of food and dress had become one of themselves. (Mildred Cable, with Francesca French, *The Gobi Desert*, Virago, 1984 edition)

In 1926, Mildred Cable and Francesca and Evangeline French left Kiayükwan Fortress, the western portal of the Great Wall of China, and became the first western women to cross the Gobi Desert.

Mildred Cable decided that she wanted to be a missionary at an early age. She set off for China in 1901 and joined Eva French at the mission in Hwochow, north-western China. There she settled with a local family to learn the language, and began her long relationship with China and the Chinese. She helped to run a mission school for young women

and a refuge for opium smokers – all part of her apprenticeship in the conversion of the Chinese to Christianity. In 1909 Eva's sister, Francesca, joined them. These three extraordinary women were almost inseparable for the rest of their lives, becoming not only missionaries but explorers.

Mildred Cable received an award from the Royal Central Asian Society for *The Gobi Desert* (1942). Among other books, often in collaboration with her friends, she wrote *Despatches from North West Kansu* (1925), *Through Jade Gate* (1927) and *A Desert Journal* (1934).

Eventually the trio bought Willow Cottage, near Shaftesbury in Dorset, and used it as a retreat, a place to recuperate and write, and a place where they could plan their next adventure.

During their travels, Mildred, Eva and Francesca had adopted a deaf and dumb Mongolian foundling. They called her Topsy, and brought her back to England. In a book that Mildred and Francesca wrote for children, called *The Story of Topsy, Little Lonely of Central Asia* (1937) they described their haven:

> When Topsy and her 'Ma-mas' are in England they spend the winter in a small London flat, but they never feel so much at home in the crowded city as they do in a certain stone cottage where they spend the summer. It is tucked away in the quietness of a Dorset land, far from any railway station.

Mildred Cable died, aged seventy-four, in London.

Willow Cottage

MARY CHANNING

c. 1687–1706
(née Brooks)
Executed: Maumbury
Rings, Dorchester

After the under-sheriff had taken some refreshment . . . [she] was brought out of prison, and dragged by her father's and her husband's houses, to the place of execution . . . She being first strangled, the fire was kindled about five in the afternoon, and in the sight of many thousands of spectators she was consumed to ashes. (Anon, *Serious Admonitions to Youth*, 1706)

These words are from a contemporary account of the execution of Mary Channing. Accused of poisoning her husband, Mary, aged about twenty, died in front of an audience of thousands at Maumbury Rings, on the south side of Dorchester. Three months earlier, in December 1705, she had given birth to a baby boy.

Mary, the daughter of Richard and Elizabeth Brooks, was born at Dorchester and given a reasonable education for a girl – she could read and write. Her parents also sent her to Exeter and London to add some sophistication and polish to a daughter of whom they were obviously proud.

Unfortunately the only description of her life from then on seems to be that of the author (suspiciously anonymous) of *Serious Admonitions to Youth, in a short account of the Life, Trial, Condemnation and Execution of Mrs Mary Channing*, published in 1706. This is such a frighteningly prejudiced piece of work, packed with moral indignation and obvious ill-will, that it is very difficult indeed to unravel any kind of truth from it.

When Mary returned to Dorchester, 'she contracted', according to this anonymous author, 'such an habit of idleness, vanity and delight in Company, that . . . she could not be made to forsake it'. At first this 'delight in company' was restricted to girlfriends and hilarious parties, but then she became interested in 'the more agreeable Conversation of the Men'. Inevitably, she fell in love – with a neighbour's son – and proceeded to hold parties in

his honour, buy him clothes, pay for his drinks and generally make rather a fool of herself.

At this point 'a Gentleman in the Town' (could this be our anonymous friend himself?) felt obliged to tell Mary's parents about her 'dissolute conduct', but they refused to believe his insinuations and told him, in no uncertain terms, to mind his own business. However, they decided that perhaps their daughter should be safely married off and chose a young man called Thomas Channing. Mary, greatly agitated, refused to co-operate. She was shut in her room for several days and when she emerged rushed straight to her lover for help. He refused to stand by her and totally rejected the idea of marriage.

Desperately unhappy, Mary decided to capitulate. In January 1704 she married Thomas Channing. It was a terrible mistake. From then on she continued not only to attend parties – and see her ex-lover – but also behaved so outrageously that even her friends were appalled.

In April 1705 she is supposed to have acquired poison from a local apothecary. Her husband, having eaten a 'dish of rice-milk' one morning, was taken ill and died five days later. Mary – rather strangely sent away by her father-in-law just *before* Thomas died – went to Somerset. She was arrested, tried and, in spite of frantic efforts by her family, she was found guilty.

Mary was allowed to stay alive until three months after the baby she expected was born. From the beginning to the end of the tragedy she insisted that she was totally innocent of the charges brought against her.

Maumbury Rings, Dorchester where Mary Channing was executed

HESTER WOLFERSTAN CHAPMAN

1899–1976
(née Pellatt)
Lived: Durnford

In reviewing her 'excellent biography' *Mary II: Queen of England* (1953), J. H. Plumb remarked that 'Miss Chapman has a rare insight into the vagaries of the human heart, a gift which academic historians all too frequently lack.' (*Times* obituary, 10 April 1976)

Hester Chapman's first novel *She Saw Them Go By*, was published in 1932 – her first historical biography, *Great Villiers*, did not appear until 1949. It was from the age of fifty that she produced her excellent and popular biographies about figures such as Lady Jane Grey, Charles II and Anne Boleyn. In 1962 her historical novel, *Eugenie*, based on the life of

Napoleon III's wife, became a best-seller.

Perhaps it was her own wide and varied experience of life that made Hester Chapman such a sensitive biographer. Born and educated in Dorset, she later worked as a fashion model in Paris, a secretary, telephonist and schoolmistress in London and as a waitress in a canteen at Combined Operations during the Second World War. Married twice, she eventually settled in Bloomsbury, London, where she continued to write. Her last book, *Four Fine Gentlemen*, was published posthumously, in 1977.

ELEANORE COADE

d. 1796

ELEANORE COADE

d. 1821
Summer residence: Lyme Regis

In Lyme Regis, a house on the corner of Pound Street and Cobb Road was once the summer residence of the Coades. The façade is decorated with their artificial stoneware, Coadestone.

The two Eleanores, mother and daughter, have, justifiably, been described as eighteenth-century industrialists and their success story began in Lyme, where the Coade family ran a pottery

business. They met, it is said, a young man, Richard Holt, who had patented a method of making artificial 'stone'. He opened a factory in Lambeth, London, but fell ill and went bankrupt. The Coades bought his factory and moved to London in 1769. The following year George Coade died and his wife, Eleanore, took over the management of the 'Artificial Stone Manufactury'. Her business methods were remarkably successful and the factory was kept at full production.

Coadestone statues, fireplaces, plaques, reliefs, urns – in fact almost every kind of artifact that could be made in this material – were sold in vast quantities, not only in Britain, but also exported abroad. The firm supplied Corinthian capitals to Boston, USA, chimney-pieces and friezes to Washington, and a statue of Nelson to Montreal, Canada, and capitals and friezes for the Royal Palace, Rio de Janeiro.

After Mrs Coade's death in 1796, her daughter, another Eleanore, became the senior partner in the firm.

Both Eleanores were buried in the Nonconformist Cemetery, Bunhill Fields, in London.

JULIANA CONINGSBY

fl. 1651
Stayed: Trent House, Trent

King Charles I was executed in 1649 and Oliver Cromwell became Lord General of the 'Commonwealth'. The heir to the throne (the future Charles II) had been removed to France but in 1650 he landed in Scotland and marched into England at the head of ten thousand men. He was defeated at the Battle of Worcester but escaped, with a price of one thousand pounds on his head.

The Battle of Worcester took place early in September 1651 and Charles eventually fled the country on 15th October. The events of those few weeks are almost unbelievably romantic and Juliana Coningsby was one of many who became involved.

Charles was passed through a complicated network of loyal supporters and friends and arrived at Trent House in Dorset, the home of Sir Francis Wyndham. It was there that he sheltered, while the next stage of his escape was discussed and planned. Charles somehow had to reach the coast and a boat to France. He was being hunted 'high and low' and so disguise was the only answer. They decided on a runaway 'marriage'. Henry, Viscount Wilmot was to play the prospective groom, Charles was to be a manservant and Juliana Coningsby, the Wyndhams' niece, was to be the eloping bride.

It must have taken a great deal of courage. Juliana rode pillion with her 'manservant' to Charmouth, where the whole party waited for a Captain Limbry, who was supposed to take them to a boat at Lyme. Limbry failed to appear and so, on 23rd September, they moved to Bridport. Bridport swarmed with Parliamentary troops and the little group rode to Broad Windsor – only to find themselves sharing lodgings with forty Parliamentary soldiers. They returned to Trent.

Charles stayed at Trent until 5th October, and was then smuggled to Heale House, near Salisbury. Juliana Coningsby, having completed her role satisfactorily, left the party before they arrived at Heale.

Charles eventually set sail from Shoreham-by-Sea and did not return to become Charles II until 1660.

Juliana married an Amias Hixt of Redlynch, in Somerset. In 1665 she petitioned for the long-promised reward for her part in the King's escape and was granted a pension of two hundred pounds.

ADELA MARION CURTIS

1864–1960

Memorial: Othona
Community Chapel,
Burton Bradstock (not
open to the public)

There can be no compromise
between Light and darkness, Good
and evil, Truth and falsehood. One
must overcome the other and make
an end of it. Darkness cannot be
overcome by darkness, evil by evil,
hatred by hatred, falsehood by
falsehood.
(Adela Curtis)

Adela Marion Curtis was born
in Japan. She died ninety-six
years later in Dorset, where
she had founded her third
spiritual centre and community at
Burton Bradstock near
Bridport.

This extraordinary woman, a
dedicated and fervent Christian,
became interested in spiritual
psychology, Eastern religions,
mysticism, meditation and the
American New Thought
movement when she was in her
thirties. From this mixture she
produced a 'practical' religious
philosophy of her own.

Having published *Janardana*, a
romance about a Punjabi princess
and her guru, in 1905, Adela
opened her first centre, 'The School
of Silence', in Kensington, London.
In 1912 she founded 'The Order of
Silence' at Coldash in Berkshire
and, in 1921, acquired about
eighteen acres of land in Dorset.
There, at St Bride's Farm, Burton
Bradstock, she founded the

'Community of Christian
Contemplatives' where her
followers lived in bungalows
growing their own food, making
their own clothes and following
the precepts of their warden and
leader, Adela Curtis.

A woman with a strong
personality as well as an excellent
mind, Adela taught, preached and
wrote. Her book *Creative Silence:
A Manual of Meditation for
Beginners in the Practice of
Transmutation of the Body* was
published in 1920. Many of her
attitudes were far ahead of her
time and still have a ring of
prophecy. When speaking on
'Meditation as a Preparation for
Post War Reconstruction' at
Oxford in 1942, she clearly stated
her distrust of woolly and idealistic
thinking and had this to say of the
future:

One truth is blazoned now in blood
and fire upon the face of the whole
earth, in warning to every nation that
the 'economic security' of material
welfare on the largest scale for
Everyman will never give humanity
freedom from fear or want or war.

Adela Curtis was cremated at
Weymouth. Her memorial is in the
Chapel of the centre she founded at
Burton Bradstock – now held by
the Othona Community.

ST CUTHBURGA

d. AD 727

Wimborne Minster

Wimborne Minster in Dorset is a
very beautiful old church and one
that has been associated with
several women over the centuries.
It is dedicated to St Cuthburga, one
of the sisters of Ina, King of the
West Saxons. She founded a
Benedictine nunnery, which
became so famous for its religious
education that it is said five
hundred women were training
there at one time. Many of them
were sent as missionaries to
Europe.

There is a window near the
north porch of the Minster which
shows St Cuthburga holding

a model of the church. She
was abbess of her nunnery
for many years and is thought to
have died about AD 727. It is
possible that she was buried in
the abbey church but, in 1013, the
nunnery was destroyed by the
Danes. Four hundred years
after St Cuthburga's death a new
church was built.

Lady Margaret Beaufort
(Henry VII's grandmother),
founded a small chapel
in the Minster in 1496, and
Elizabeth I granted a Charter of
Rights and Property almost a
hundred years later.

QUEEN ELFRIDA

fl. AD 978
Lived: Corfe Castle

In AD 975 the Saxon King, Edgar, died. He had been married twice and his eldest son, Edward, by his first marriage, became King, as was his right. This left Edgar's widow, Elfrida, and their son Ethelred, aged about ten.

It is said that Elfrida became obsessed by the desire that *her* son should reign over Wessex. Only King Edward, her stepson, stood in the way.

One day Edward, out hunting, decided to visit his stepmother at her home, Corfe Castle in Dorset. Elfrida met him at the castle gate:

> On his arrival, alluring him to her with female blandishments, she made him lean forward, and after saluting him while he was eagerly drinking from the cup which had been presented, the dagger of an attendant pierced him through. (William of Malmesbury, *Chronicle of the Kings of England*, 1847 edition)

The story goes that Elfrida attempted to hide his body in a well. It is also said that when she rode in state to Edward's eventual tomb (at Shaftesbury), her horse came to a halt and refused to approach the grave. A little later Elfrida retired to a nunnery at Wherwell (Hampshire), leaving her son Ethelred as King. He reigned for thirty-seven years.

Commemorative sign in Corfe

MARY FRAMPTON

1773–1846
Lived: Moreton House, Moreton

I was dressed as a grown-up person for the first time, and wore powder, then the mark of distinction of womanhood. My dress was a black body and pink slip, with a crape petticoat, ornamented with pink bows, puffings, etc., and feathers in my head. (*The Journal of Mary Frampton: 1779–1846*, 1885)

The journals or diaries of women in the past were often packed with delightful detail and brought ordinary, domestic events into sharp focus – Mary Frampton's journal was no exception.

Born in Dorset, Mary lived at Moreton, north-east of Weymouth, and kept an erratic journal from 1779 to 1846. Most of her descriptions were of social occasions, family weddings and fashions:

At that time everybody wore powder and pomatum; a large triangular thing called a cushion, to which the hair was frizzed up with three or four enormous curls on each side; the higher the pyramid of hair, gauze, feathers, and other ornaments was carried the more fashionable it was thought.

Occasionally, however, she touches on more serious events, when the peace of the countryside was disturbed:

At Sherborne [Dorset] a considerable mob assembled. They proceeded to Sherborne Castle – Lord Digby's – where they broke every pane of glass which they could get at, and tried to force the great gates leading into the court.

Mary Frampton died in Dorchester in 1846.

TRYPHENA GALE

1851–1890?
(née Sparks)
Lived: Puddletown

THOUGHTS OF PH-A:

Not a line of her writing have I
Not a thread of her hair,
No mark of her late time as dame
  in her dwelling whereby
  I may picture her there;
And in vain do I urge my unsight
  To conceive my lost prize
At her close, whom I knew when her
  dreams were upbrimming with
  light
And with laughter her eyes.
(Thomas Hardy, *Wessex Poems*,
1898)

Tryphena Sparks, of Puddletown near Dorchester met Thomas Hardy when she was sixteen. He had just returned to Dorset from London, an enthusiastic young architect. They fell in love and became engaged.

It has been suggested that Tryphena became pregnant and that Hardy's mother then told her son that he could not possibly marry her. Tryphena, it seems, was his mother's illegitimate granddaughter. There was so muc secrecy at this point that it is difficult to unravel any exact sequence of events. However, Tryphena left Puddletown at the age of eighteen and enrolled at Stockwell Teacher Training College, in London. Two years later she became headmistress of the Public Free School in Plymouth, Devon, where she met Charles Gale and married him. Sh had four children, lived at 13 Fore Street in Topsham near Exeter and died there, aged only thirty-nine.

Thomas Hardy married Emma Lavinia Gifford (q.v.), in 1874, bu it is thought that his novel *The Return of the Native* (1878) was the story of his love for Tryphena Sparks.

ELIZABETH HAM

1783–?
Born: North Perrott

One whole Book finished before I am out of my teens. Early memories seem rife, but I fear little profitable. We live a large portion of our lives between fifteen and twenty-five. (Eric Gillett (ed.), *Elizabeth Ham, 1783–1820*, 1945)

Elizabeth Ham wrote a diary that is a simple, straightforward and touching account of a young woman's life at the turn of the eighteenth century.

Born at North Perrott, on the Dorset-Somerset border, Elizabeth first went to school in Dorchester. She was staying at Weymouth when the King, (George III), and other members of the Royal family visited the town:

While the King never seemed afraid of the weather the Queen and Princesses always wore dark blue habits on these occasions and I have often seen them look very miserable and bedraggled on their return.

Elizabeth moved to Ireland wit her family but returned to the We Country to work as a governess i Bath. She found the experience so dreadful, however, that she left after a year. Her attempt to start school of her own in Dorchester failed and Elizabeth was forced to become a governess again, this time in Clifton, Bristol. At this crucial moment her diary ends. N account of the rest of her life has s far been traced.

FLORENCE HARDY

1879–1937
(née Dugdale)
Buried: St Michael's
Churchyard, Stinsford

In 1906 Florence Dugdale (aged twenty-seven), a teacher and hopeful writer, met Thomas Hardy (aged sixty-six), the novelist. She offered to help with the checking and revision of Part Three of his epic drama, *The Dynasts*. They became friends and, helped by Hardy, Florence published her story 'The Apotheosis of the Minx' in the *Cornhill Magazine*. In 1908 she gave up teaching, worked for pictorial weekly called *The Spher* and continued to see a great deal Hardy. She also began to write stories for children.

In 1910 Florence met Hardy's wife, Emma (q.v.) at the Lyceum Club in London and was invited t their home, Max Gate, just outsid

Dorchester. Two years later she published *In Lucy's Garden*, and Emma Hardy died. Florence moved into Max Gate and in 1914 married Thomas Hardy.

It was not a happy marriage. Although Thomas and his first wife had barely been speaking to each other before her death, as soon as Emma died he became haunted and obsessed by memories of their life together. Florence was disappointed, lonely and neglected.

She published *A Book of Baby Pets* in 1915.

Thomas Hardy died in 1928 and his second wife became a wealthy widow. She revised his autobiography and then began to make a life of her own.

Florence Hardy was involved in many local philanthropic activities. She died in 1937, aged fifty-eight, and her ashes were buried in Stinsford Churchyard.

St Michael's Churchyard, Stinsford, the burial place of Florence Hardy

HANNAH HEWLING

1662–1732
(Mrs Henry Cromwell)
Buried her brother at
Lyme Regis

In 1685 King Charles II died and his brother, James II, ascended the throne. James had previously embraced Catholicism openly and was not at all popular with a large number of his subjects. Within six months of his accession the Duke of Monmouth, an illegitimate son of Charles II, landed at Lyme in Dorset and began to recruit an army.

Proclaimed 'King' at Taunton in Somerset, Monmouth and his followers fought the forces of James II at the Battle of Sedgemoor. They were totally defeated and the rebellion was crushed. Monmouth was captured, refused a pardon, and executed.

Then came retribution, Judge Jeffreys and the Bloody Assizes. Trials were held in the West Country and hundreds of those who had joined the rebellion were transported. Others were fined, flogged, died in prison or were horribly executed.

Among those condemned to death were two young brothers, Benjamin Hewling, aged twenty-two, and William Hewling, aged nineteen. William was tried at Dorchester and executed at Lyme. Benjamin was tried and executed at Taunton. Their sister, Hannah, made valiant attempts to save them:

The father of this unfortunate family was dead; the mother, from her distress, incapable of acting . . . the other sisters were hardly out of their childhood, it fell upon this young lady alone to conduct the whole affair, in the prison for their comfort, and with the Court for their pardon. (John Hutchins, *The History and Antiquities of Dorset*, 1774)

With enormous courage she followed her brothers through every stage of their ordeal. She went to London to petition the King, but was told by Lord Churchill that she was wasting her time: 'For that marble is as capable of feeling compassion as the King's heart.' She tried to make sure that her brothers were reasonably comfortable in prison and she begged Judge Jeffreys for their lives. They were both executed.

Hannah paid the Judge one thousand pounds before Benjamin died at Lyme. As a result, he was allowed a normal burial in the churchyard instead of having his remains hung in the town. Large crowds attended the funeral. The same routine followed William's execution at Taunton.

The following year Hannah Hewling married Major Henry Cromwell. She had eight sons and two daughters and, not at all surprisingly, became known for her radical political and religious opinions.

She died aged seventy and was buried in the Nonconformist burial ground, Bunhill Fields, in London.

LUCY KEMP-WELCH

1869–1958

Born: Bournemouth

Like most artists who came to maturity and were established before the end of the nineteenth century, Lucy Kemp-Welch suffered somewhat in her later reputation from the violent changes in art which followed. In her prime as an animal painter she held a position in this country comparable to that of Rosa Bonheur in France. (*Times* obituary, 1958)

Lucy Kemp-Welch was born in Bournemouth and became a painter of animals, particularly horses, and country subjects. She was educated mainly at home but studied art at Professor Herkomer's School at Bushey near London. Herkomer had this to say of his ex-pupil:

> When I started the Herkomer School I made a point of giving the female students the same chance as the male students. The curious result has been after twenty-one years, that a woman has to be proclaimed the most successful.

Lucy Kemp-Welch was a sensitive and dedicated artist who went to great lengths to ensure that her paintings were technically correct, as well as emotionally inspired. For her picture *The Incoming Tide*, a painting of seagulls swooping down to the ocean with cliffs behind, she stood for hours waist-deep in the sea, working on studies of birds.

She was the first President of the Society of Animal Painters, a member of the Royal Society of British Artists and in 1917 was elected a member of the Royal Institute of Oil Painters.

ELIZABETH LOVELESS

1800–1868
(née Snook Sprachlen)

Born: Dewlish
Lived: Tolpuddle

In May 1834, just before being transported as a convict to Van Dieman's Land, George Loveless, of Tolpuddle in Dorset, wrote to his wife, Elizabeth:

> I thank you, my dear wife, for the kind attention you have ever paid me, and you may safely rely upon it that as long as I live it will be my constant endeavour to return that kindness in every possible way . . . Don't send me any money to distress yourself. I shall do well, for He who is Lord of the winds and waves will be my support in life and death.

George Loveless was one of the six farm labourers of Tolpuddle who were convicted at the Dorchester Assizes, 'for administering unlawful oaths', (in fact, attempting to organize a union). The savagery of the punishment meted out to them – seven years' transportation – caused such a storm of protest that the men were given a full pardon and eventually, after three long years, returned home. Meanwhile, their wives, mothers, sisters and sweethearts had had to manage the best they could.

Elizabeth, who came from Dewlish near Tolpuddle, had married George Loveless, farm-worker and Methodist preacher, in 1824, and had three children. One can only imagine her feelings when her husband was condemned to seven years' transportation. While George was in Dorchester Gaol she was refused permission to visit him and matters

were made worse by a local magistrate, James Frampton, who refused to grant parish relief to the dependants of all six men.

Fortunately for all the women concerned, the news of this injustice provoked the unions to action. Subscriptions poured in from the coach painters, tailors, shipwrights, silk weavers, journeymen, gardeners, and many other unions. The money received was collected and distributed to the wives and families while they were in need.

Elizabeth's husband arrived back in London, a free man, on 13 June 1837. In 1844 the family emigrated to Canada and eventually settled in Siloam, near London, Ontario. It is there, in Siloam cemetery, that Elizabeth Loveless is buried.

ELIZABETH MUNTZ

894–1977

Buried: Chaldon Herring (East Chaldon) Churchyard

Elizabeth Muntz and her sister, Hope (q.v.) were both born in Toronto, Canada. They were descendants of the Muntz family of Warwickshire, England, and their great-grandfather, George Frederick Muntz MP, was one of the early campaigners for the abolition of child labour.

Elizabeth studied at the Ontario College of Art and also in Paris. Although she occasionally painted in oil and tempera, she became first and foremost a sculptor, working in stone, bronze and wood. She exhibited in London and abroad.

When she died in 1977 she had lived and worked for about forty

Appliqué nativity in the church at Chaldon Herring (East Chaldon), designed by Elizabeth Muntz

years in Dorset. She was buried in the churchyard of Chaldon Herring (East Chaldon). Inside the church, when we visited, was a delightful appliqué nativity picture, in the children's corner. A small notice nearby explained its presence:

This picture was designed by Elizabeth Muntz in the 1940 war for the children of the village who worked on it with her in her studio. She cut out all the animals, who were local characters, and the children stitched them on. The background shows the Tumuli known as The Five Marys.

ISABELLE HOPE MUNTZ

1907–1981
Buried: Chaldon Herring (East Chaldon) Churchyard

In the work for which she will be most widely and fondly remembered, *The Golden Warrior*, her deep love for the England of the Dorset hills and lanes she knew so well showed clearly, and her complete mastery of the 'sage-style' of writing. She was a consummate mistress of English. (*Times* obituary, 5 October 1981)

Hope Muntz, like her elder sister, Elizabeth (q.v.), was born in Toronto, Canada. Although she also studied Art in both Toronto and London (and at one time even worked at aircraft engineering), Hope became not an artist or a sculptor but a writer and scholar, specializing particularly in the Norman Conquest of 1066. She wrote and reviewed under the

pseudonym William Langland, but her story of Harold and William, *The Golden Warrior*, was published under her own name in 1948.

Hope Muntz was elected a Fellow of the Society of Antiquaries of London in 1969 and a Fellow of the Royal Historical Society in 1972. She wrote a script for 'The Norman Conquest in the Bayeaux Tapestry' in 1966 and was preparing a television version of *The Golden Warrior* just before her death. She was buried, not far from her sister, in the beautiful little churchyard of Chaldon Herring (East Chaldon) in Dorset.

ELIZABETH MAUD PEPPERELL

1914–1971
(Mrs Brewin)
Lived: Pepperell House, Shaftesbury

At a thanksgiving service for Elizabeth Pepperell in London, John Marsh, Director-General of the British Institute of Management, gave an address. He quoted from letters about Elizabeth: 'Just to see her coming towards one was a liberation'; 'She had an unquenchable faith in the essential goodness of mankind, and a deep sympathy for the difficulties of women in industry'. He also mentioned her life outside London, 'In recent years – her joy at discovering Shaftesbury and Dorset – at weekends. There with Paul she planned to spend her retiring years – but alas it was an unrealized dream. In Shaftesbury, this day, there are many who share our thanksgiving'.

When her children were small, Elizabeth bought Abbey Stone, Shaftesbury, as a weekend home. Later, she and her husband moved to Avishays, which was larger and

had a beautiful garden. After her death, the Abbeyfield Society bought the house and named it Pepperell House. It was turned into an old people's home.

Elizabeth Pepperell was a most unusual woman. She was born in Poplar, East London, and left school when she was fourteen, becoming a packer and then supervisor at Bryant & May's match factory. Determined to understand the causes of industrial conflict, she took evening classes in industrial history and economics and was eventually awarded a scholarship to the London School of Economics. In 1940 she was appointed Chief Personnel Officer for Carreras Ltd – a factory with three thousand employees. In 1951 she married Paul Brewin and, in 1952, she joined the Industrial Society as their first woman assistant director. She held this position for the rest of her life.

ELIZABETH PHILPOT
1780–1857
MARY PHILPOT
1777–1838
MARGARET PHILPOT
?–1845
Philpot Museum, Lyme Regis

In dedicating this species to Miss Philpot, I have pleasure in publicly recognising the services which she has rendered to palaeontology and notably to fossil ichthyology, by the care she has taken in collecting the fossil remains of the Lias at Lyme Regis. The species which we have just described and which is in her collection can be regarded as one of the finest fishes of this formation. (J. L. R. Agassiz, *Recherches sur les Poissons Fossiles*, 1833/44)

The Miss Philpot referred to by the Swiss geologist, Jean Agassiz, was Elizabeth Philpot, one of the four Philpot sisters who came to live in Lyme Regis, Dorset, in about 1805. Three of them, Elizabeth, Mary and Margaret, remained there for the rest of their lives and the collection of fossils they eventually made was presented to Oxford University in 1880.

Although Elizabeth was obviously the presiding genius, all three sisters co-operated enthusiastically in this fascinating hobby. They not only collected fossils, but dissected marine invertebrates and examined them under the microscope; they also owned a fossil-cabinet, built up a library and corresponded with leading scientists of the day. Among their many friends and acquaintances were Henry Thomas De La Beche, Richard Owen, William Buckland and Jean Agassiz. The Philpot sisters also knew, and worked with, Mary Anning (q.v.).

Although these remarkable sisters made a fossil collection of great scientific interest, after Elizabeth's death in 1857, they were soon forgotten. Their name is remembered only by the Philpot collection at Oxford and the Philpot Museum in Lyme Regis.

ELIZABETH, LADY RALEGH
1565?–1647
(née Throckmorton)
Lived: Sherborne Castle

Sherborne Castle in Dorset was once the home of Sir Walter Ralegh and his wife Elizabeth, or Bess, as she was known.

Ralegh, explorer, scientist, pirate and poet was a favourite of Queen Elizabeth I, and it was at her court that he met and fell in love with Bess Throckmorton, one of the maids-of-honour. Rashly, the two lovers married secretly, probably some time in 1592, and when the Queen was told they were promptly sent to the Tower of London for a few months. On their release they left for Sherborne and started their married life in the home that the Queen had given Ralegh earlier that year. It was at Sherborne that Bess gave birth to a son, christened Walter after his father.

Although Ralegh was eventually forgiven by the Queen, his wife was never readmitted to court and spent most of her time in Dorset.

In 1603 Elizabeth I died and James VI of Scotland became James I of England. Ralegh, who was opposed to the succession, was suspected of plotting against the King and was tried for conspiracy and treason. He spent the next twelve years in the Tower. Bess and their son Wat were allowed to live there with him and in 1605 a second son, Carew, was born.

One of the worst things that happened at this time was the loss of their beloved home. Bess petitioned and fought fiercely to retain Sherborne but in 1607 she finally lost the battle.

In 1616 Ralegh was released from prison and allowed to lead an expedition in search of gold. He took Wat with him. The expedition was a failure and young Wat was killed during a clash with the Spaniards.

Bess met her husband on his return to Plymouth in June 1618. In October he was condemned to death and executed. His wife, the night before his death, wrote in desperation to her brother:

I desire, good brother, that you will be pleased to let me bury the worthy body of my noble husband, Sir

**Sherborne Castle where
Elizabeth, Lady Ralegh
lived**

Walter Ralegh, in your church at
Beddington . . . The Lords have given
me his dead body, though they
denied me his life. This night he shall
be brought you with two or three of
my men. Let me hear presently. God
hold me in my wits.

Bess was not, in fact, allowed
her husband's body, only his head.
She is said to have had it embalmed
and to have carried it around with
her to her dying day in a leather
bag.

ROSE RENDALL

1887–1958
Philpot Museum, Lyme
Regis

Rose Rendall, daughter of the
mayor of Lyme Regis, sat for
James McNeill Whistler in 1895,
when she was eight years old and
he was nearly seventy.

Whistler, who was visiting Lyme
at the time, looked out of a
window one day and noticed a
remarkably beautiful little girl
walking past. When he went up to
her in the street and asked if he
could paint her, Rose fled in horror
– convinced that this strange old
man intended to cover her with
paint. The misunderstanding

satisfactorily explained, she sat for
him at 51 Broad Street. The
portrait, now in the United States,
was called *Little Rose of Lyme*.

Rose grew up, went to Exeter to
learn millinery and then married a
Mr Herridge. In the Philpot
Museum at Lyme Regis we found a
small glass case, where one or two
of her belongings are displayed and
her story briefly told. There is also
a photograph of Rose as a young
woman, looking confident, elegant
– and still remarkably beautiful.

MARIE STOPES

1880–1958

Holiday home: Upper
Lighthouse, Portland Bill

This Museum is a gift to the People of Portland Island, the houses and ground presented by Dr Marie Stopes and the money for their restoration and equipment collected by Public Subscription. (Plaque in the Portland Museum, Easton, Dorset.)

The museum at Easton is small but fascinating. Opened in 1929, 'the project being largely due to the generosity and interest of Dr Marie Stopes', it is based in what was known as Avice's Cottage, the name taken from Thomas Hardy's heroine, Avice Caro, in his novel *The Well-Beloved*.

Marie Stopes always loved this part of Dorset. After her second marriage, to Humphrey Verdon Roe, she and her husband acquired as a holiday home one of the lighthouses on Portland Bill. It was there, she claimed, that her son, Harry, was conceived.

Marie Stopes, born in Edinburgh, entered University College, London, in 1900. In 1905 she became the youngest Doctor of Science in England, specializing in

Palaeobotany (the study of fossil plants). She married R. R. Gates in 1911 but, five years later, the marriage was annulled . . . Marie was still a virgin. Her book *Married Love*, was first published in 1918, the twenty-eighth edition appearing in 1955. In her author's preface she wrote:

In my first marriage I paid such a terrible price for sex-ignorance that I feel that knowledge gained at such a cost should be placed at the service of humanity.

Marie was a highly controversial figure. With her second husband she opened a birth control clinic in North London, offering free advice to married women. When her son Harry was born *The Times* refused to print an announcement of the birth.

Dr Marie Stopes died of cancer in 1958. She was cremated at Golders Green in London, but her ashes were scattered into the sea at Portland Bill.

CAROLA THÖRSANDER

1898–1984
The Book in Hand,
Shaftesbury

From 1968 to 1980 the manager of the bookshop The Book in Hand in Shaftesbury was Carola Thörsander. The daughter of a Swedish father and an English mother, Carola was brought up in Italy and eventually spoke five languages. The author, Christopher Driver, owner of The Book in Hand, said of her experiences during the Second World War:

She and her sister must have been a little like Swedish versions of the Mitford sisters. The sister married a high-ranking Nazi and lived in a schloss. Carola was caught in south Germany with her mother . . . and played the opposite role, feeding and, towards the end, harbouring prisoners of war, protected by her Swedish passport (she refused to put up the obligatory portrait of Hitler in her house unless her enemy the local schoolmaster put up the picture of the King of Sweden in his).

After the war Carola was recruited as an interpreter by the Americans, to help in the interrogation of war criminals. It was after this that she moved to England and settled in Dorset. She was seventy when she became manager of The Book in Hand.

SYLVIA TOWNSEND WARNER

1893–1978

Buried: St Nicholas Churchyard, Chaldon Herring (East Chaldon)

Although Sylvia Townsend Warner was born at Harrow-on-the-Hill, she lived and worked for most of her life in Dorset. Her father was a housemaster at Harrow School but Sylvia later remarked that she hadn't really been educated: 'I was very lucky'! During the First World War she worked in a munitions factory and then spent ten years as one of the editors of *Tudor Church Music*, a ten-volume work published by Oxford University Press. Her first novels, *Lolly Willowes* (1926) and *Mr Fortune's Maggot* (1927) established her as a writer of unusual ability. Many of her short stories appeared in the *New Yorker*, and her biography of T. H. White (1967) was considered outstanding. Her *Letters*, edited by William Maxwell, were published in 1982.

Sylvia Townsend Warner's great friend and companion was Valentine Ackland (q.v.). They met in Dorset and decided to live together, settling near Maiden Newton. After Valentine Ackland's death in 1969 Sylvia continued to live there:

It is no time of year . . . The grass is as green as grass, the skies are high and fathomless. The birds are singing. This morning the first aconite bloomed in the path. I do not feel as graceful as the landscape. My legs are like ancient monuments, they ache and give way, and my cats look at me deploringly and say privately to each other that I am a shadow of my old self. (*Letters*, 1982)

She died the year she wrote this letter to William Maxwell and was buried with Valentine Ackland in the churchyard at Chaldon Herring (East Chaldon).

Sylvia Townsend Warner buried with Valentine Ackland (q.v.) in St Nicholas Churchyard, Chaldon Herring (East Chaldon)

JULIA AUGUSTA WEBSTER

1837–1894
(née Davies)
Born: Poole

In 1879 a book called *A Housewife's Opinions* was published. It was a collection of articles, mainly about the status and education of women, written by Augusta Webster for *The Examiner*, a well-known weekly journal. Her 'opinions' were strongly held, clearly expressed and often wittily presented.

Augusta was not only an early feminist and educationalist, she was also a brilliant linguist, a playwright and an excellent poet.

Born in Poole, Dorset, she later lived in Cambridge, and it was there that she attended classes at the Cambridge School of Art and also studied Greek. Her first volume of poetry, *Blanche Lisle, and other Poems*, was published in 1860 under the pseudonym Cecil Home.

In 1863 she married Thomas Webster, fellow of Trinity College, Cambridge, and three years later had produced not only a daughter, but a translation into English verse of *The Prometheus Bound* by Aeschylus and a volume of her own poetry, called *Dramatic Studies*. The Websters moved to London in 1870. A collection of her poems, called *Portraits*, published that year, went into a second edition. *Portraits* contained one of her outstanding poems, *The Castaway*, which follows the thoughts of a high-class prostitute as she turns the pages of the diary she kept when young:

Poor little diary, with its simple
  thoughts,
Its good resolves, its 'Studied French
  an hour',
'Read Modern History', 'Trimmed
  up my grey hat',
'Darned stockings', 'Tatted',
  'Practised my new song',
'Went to the daily service', 'Took
  Bess soup',
'Went out to tea'. Poor simple diary!
And did *I* write it? Was I this good
  girl,
This budding colourless young rose
  of home?
Did I so live content in such a life,
Seeing no larger scope, nor asking it.

Augusta died in London. Her work did not continue to receive the attention it most certainly deserved. As *The Castaway* drily remarked:

Well, well, the silly rules this silly
  world
makes about women!

SOMERSET

ELIZABETH OGILVY BENGER
1778–1827
Born: Wells

She has been heard to relate, that in the tormenting want of books which she suffered during her childhood, it was one of her resources to plant herself at the window of the only bookseller's shop in the place, to read the open pages of the new publications there displayed, and to return again, day after day, to examine whether, by good fortune, a leaf of any of them might have been turned over. (Lucy Aikin, 1827)

Elizabeth Benger was born at Wells in Somerset but, when she was only four years old, her father decided rather late in life to join the Navy and moved his wife and daughter to Kent. It was there that Elizabeth began to show a precocious interest in literature and, when she was only twelve, her mother took the unusual step of sending her daughter to a boys' school to learn Latin. When she was thirteen Elizabeth produced her first poem, The Female Geniad.

In 1796, Mr Benger died in the East Indies. His wife and eighteen-year-old daughter moved to Wiltshire, where they suffered all the humiliations of genteel poverty, until Elizabeth persuaded her mother that they should move to London. There Elizabeth introduced herself to various well-known figures of the literary and artistic world and eventually became friendly with the Lambs, Elizabeth Inchbald, the Porter sisters (q.v.) and the Aikin family.

In 1809 her long poem, On the Slave Trade, was published, illustrated by Robert Smirke, R.A. She also wrote two novels, Marian and The Heart and the Fancy, but it was not until she turned to historical biography that Elizabeth really felt at home. In quick succession she produced the 'Memoirs' of Mrs Elizabeth Hamilton (1818), John Tobin (1820), Anne Boleyn (1821), Mary Queen of Scots (1823) and Elizabeth of Bohemia (1825). She was working on the memoirs of Henry IV of France when she died, aged forty-nine.

SARAH BIFFIN (OR BEFFIN)
1784–1850
Born: East Quantoxhead

The baby born to the Biffins in 1784 at East Quantoxhead, Somerset, was terribly disabled. She had no arms and, although later descriptions are confused, she may also have had no proper legs. They christened her Sarah.

Sarah's parents were poor. They must have been exceptionally loving and patient for, without help from anyone else, their daughter not only survived, but learnt to write, sew and paint. Most of this she achieved by using her mouth.

In her twenties, Sarah was 'discovered' by a Mr Dukes. Before long she had signed a contract with him and Mr Dukes proceeded to exhibit her round the country. She was billed as 'The Astonishing Curiosity . . . only thirty-seven inches high'. Sarah sat in 'a commodious booth' and, in front of a gawping public who had paid at least sixpence for the privilege, she sewed, painted miniatures and signed autographs. Her 'impresario' offered a thousand guineas to anyone who could prove that she was incapable of fulfilling the claims made in his advertisement.

Sarah is said to have 'performed' for sixteen years, before she was noticed by the Earl of Morton,

The Nobility, Ladies and Gentlemen, are respecy...y informed
that the astonishing Curiosity,

Miss BEFFIN,

Intends exhibiting her wonderful Powers

IN A COMMODIOUS BOOTH
During the Race Week.

THIS YOUNG LADY was born deficient of Arms, Hands,
and Legs; she is of a comely Appearance, twenty-five Years of
Age, and only thirty-seven Inches high. She displays a great
Genius, and is an admirer of the fine Arts; but what renders her
so worthy of public Notice is the industrious and astonishing
Means she has invented and practised in obtaining the Use of the
Needle, Scissars, Pen, Pencil, &c. wherein she is extremely adroit.
She can cut out and make any part of her own Cloaths, sews,
extremely neat and in a most wonderful manner, writes well,
draws Landscapes, paints Miniatures, and many more wonderful
Things, all of which she does principally with

HER MOUTH.

The Reader may easily think it impossible she should be capable
of doing what is inserted in this Bill; but if she cannot, and even
much more, the conductor will forfeit

1000 GUINEAS.

Open from Twelve o'Clock in the Forenoon.

PIT, 1s. GALLERY, 6d.

N. B. Miniature Likenesses printed on Ivory at Three Guineas
each.

who promptly came to her rescue.
She was adopted by the aristocracy
and taught by Mr Craig, a
professional artist. Suddenly she
became famous and fashionable,
even the Royal family patronized
her, and in 1821 she received a
medal from the Society of Artists.
She was thirty-seven.

Sarah Biffin eventually retired to
Liverpool. She would have died in
extreme poverty if an unknown Mr
Rathbone had not organized a
pension on her behalf. She died,
aged sixty-six, and, in 1925,
Liverpool paid a tribute to her
memory by holding an exhibition
of her work.

Fairground bill for Sarah Biffin

MARGARET GRACE BONDFIELD

1873–1953
Born: near Chard

Margaret Bondfield became
Britain's first woman Cabinet
Minister in 1929. She was fifty-six.

Born near Chard, in Somerset,
she was one of the younger
children in a working-class family
of seven sons and four daughters.
Her father was a lace-maker and
the family was poor. Margaret left
school when she was fourteen and
worked in Brighton as a shop girl.
Three years later she moved to
London and became a member of
the London District Council of the
Shop Assistants Union (SAU).

Politically aroused, Margaret
helped the trades unionist, Mary
Macarthur, to found the National
Federation of Women Workers.
Elected to the TUC General

Council in 1918, she attended the
Berne Socialist Conference a
year later, became MP for
Northampton in 1923 and, in
1924, was made Parliamentary
Secretary to the Ministry of
Labour. Five years later she herself
became Minister of the
department.

In an article in the *Daily Herald*
(1931) Harold Laski, although
highly critical of Margaret
Bondfield's policies, praised what
he considered to be the secret of
her success – eloquence:

Miss Bondfield has what perhaps I
may call the Albert Hall mind at its
best. She has the gift for that
passionate oratory which captures
the emotions of an audience and

118

sweeps it along with her . . . She is the revivalist in politics. She does not argue, she seeks to lift you out of yourself. She feels the truth of her convictions from within; and she communicates the warmth of her own internal fire to her audience.

The Rt. Hon. Margaret Bondfield's book, *A Life's Work*, was published in 1950. She died in Surrey and was cremated at Golders Green, in London.

MARY BRIDGE
fl. 1685
Admiral Blake Museum,
Bridgwater

In the Admiral Blake Museum at Bridgwater, Somerset, there is a short, but deadly-looking sword. It is said to be the weapon which Mary Bridge used to stab and kill a Royalist officer in 1685.

Unfortunately, in the Somerset County Museum at Taunton, there is *another* short sword and that, too, is said to be the one used by Mary Bridge.

Luckily, the story which makes the sword so important is not in dispute. It begins during the Monmouth Rebellion in 1685, when Charles II's illegitimate son, the handsome young Duke of Monmouth, challenged the King's right to the throne (the King was the unpopular James II, and was Monmouth's uncle). Monmouth's 'rebels' – most of them recruited in the West Country – were defeated at the Battle of Sedgemoor, in Somerset, and the frightful punishment of those who had taken part in the rebellion began immediately.

The Bridge family lived at Weston Zoyland, a village on the plain of Sedgemoor, in a house called Weston Court. The King's commander-in-chief Lord Feversham, chose their home as headquarters for his men and the Bridges were compelled to offer hospitality.

After the battle Lord Feversham was involved in the trials and executions of the rebels and one day he departed for Taunton, leaving his troop of soldiers behind at Weston Court. The men, bored and unoccupied, consumed large quantities of cider. Some of them forced their way into the house, where they found the women alone and unprotected, among them Mrs Bridge and her twelve-year-old daughter, Mary.

What followed has been politely described as an incident in which one of the soldiers 'insulted the lady of the house'. Quite clearly it was an attempted rape. Twelve-year-old Mary Bridge, seeing her mother attacked, snatched the sword from the soldier's belt and killed him with it. She was promptly arrested and taken to Taunton, where she was tried before a Colonel Kirke.

Mary was given an honourable acquittal and the Colonel presented her with the sword she had used to protect her mother. So it came to be passed down through the family, until a Miss Mary Bridge, of Taunton, showed it to the Somerset Archaeological Society in 1862. Many years later the sword arrived at the Museum in Bridgwater . . . or Taunton.

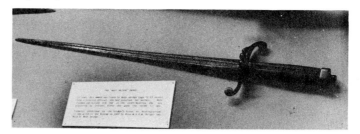

One of the Mary Bridge Swords at the Admiral Blake Museum, Bridgwater

CATCOTT CHURCH AND ADVICE TO WOMEN

St Peter's Church, Catcott

Tucked away in the village of Catcott, Somerset, is the beautiful, fifteenth-century church of St Peter's, and painted on the walls inside are several mural texts in Gothic script. Two of these are words from the 'Letter to Titus' and are very unusual, as they are directed at the 'aged' men and women of the congregation.

The murals are obviously of a great age, and one imagines that, hundreds of years ago, a vicar of

Catcott decided that the elders of the village needed a stern reminder of their responsibilities. The 'aged men' are requested to be sober, grave and patient; the text directed at the women is a little longer:

The aged women likewise that they be in behaviour as becometh holiness, not false accusers, teachers of good things, that they may teach the young women to be sober, to be chaste, keepers at home, to love their husbands. (Titus ii. 3, 4, 5)

Mural text in St Peter's Church, Catcott

ANN ESTELLA, VISCOUNTESS CAVE

1855–1938
(née Penfold)
Buried: St Mary's Church, Berrow

Lady Cave was born in Chard, Somerset. She married in 1885 and her husband, Viscount Cave, later became Lord Chancellor of England (1922–1928). A lively, unconventional and artistic woman, she was known as a splendid hostess and made an enormous number of friends in both literary and political circles.

In 1928 she published *Three Journeys*, based on the diaries she had kept when visiting East Africa, South Africa, Canada and the United States. The following year she expanded a short, autobiographical piece she had written for the *Cornhill Magazine* into a book, *Odds and Ends of My Life*. Then, in 1933, came *Ant Antics*, an amusing collection of poems, stories, essays and 'thoughts' about ants. Estella Cave did much of the writing – and all the delightful illustrations. She had persuaded many of her friends, including Beverly Nichols, J. M. Barrie and Stanley Baldwin, to make contributions; Laurence Housman wrote this poem for her:

ANN ESTELLA CAVE

Here is Ann Estella Cave
Telling me how Ants behave.
In my heart I have to quell a
Rising Doubt in Ann Estella
From a fear that – if I can't
She'll depict me as an ant.
Therefore – O Estella Ann,
I'll believe you – if I *can*!

She lived for many years at Burnham-on-Sea, in Somerset and was buried with her husband in the churchyard of St Mary's, Berrow.

ALICE CLARK

1874–1934
Greenbank Swimming Pool, Street

Alice Clark was born in Street, Somerset. Her family owned C. & J. Clark's Shoe Factory there and Alice decided to make the family business her career. She left school in 1893, took a course in housewifery at Bristol and then returned to Street to begin her apprenticeship:

Her father not only made the arrangements for her to learn the technique of shoemaking in these early days, but by his backing during the following years he gave her the chance to rise to high responsibility which is very rarely given to a woman even now, and was then almost unheard of. (M. C. Gillett, *Alice Clark*)

After a serious illness in 1897,

Alice went back to the factory, took charge of the machine room, and became one of the directors. In 1909 she fell ill again, and this time took longer to recover. A few years later she settled temporarily in London and joined the executive of the Union of Suffrage Societies.

In 1918, Alice was awarded Mrs Bernard Shaw's scholarship for the investigation of women's historic past and became a student at the London School of Economics and in 1919 her book *Working Life of Women in the 17th Century* was published. Then she joined the London committee of the Society of Friends helping to organize relief work in Austria.

In 1922 Alice returned to Somerset and picked up the threads at the factory in Street. Apart from helping with the daily administration of the business, she also undertook personnel management and was an enthusiastic supporter of a non-contributory pension scheme which was to give retirement pensions to the factory employees at the age of sixty-five. At the same time she cared for her elderly parents who were living at Mill Field. She died, aged sixty, and left enough money to provide the Greenbank Swimming Pool in Street.

Monument to Alice Clark outside Greenbank Swimming Pool in Street

AVERIL COLBY

1900–1983
Lived: Langford

Averil Colby who lived for many years in Langford, Somerset, was not only an expert needlewoman but a writer and historian of needlework, particularly patchwork. Her attractive and inspiring book, *Patchwork*, was published in 1958 and was directly responsible for the enormous upsurge of interest in patchwork in the 1950s and 1960s. One of her best-known designs was the velvet and satin patchwork cope, which was made by the parishioners of Burford, Oxfordshire, to commemorate the Coronation of the present Queen.

ELIZABETH, LADY DRAKE

fl. 1585
(née Sydenham)
Lived: Combe Sydenham Hall, Monksilver

Elizabeth Sydenham became the second wife of the great Elizabethan seafarer, Sir Francis Drake. She was born at Combe Sydenham, near Monksilver in Somerset and was the only daughter of Sir George Sydenham.

Drake's courtship of Elizabeth was not a great success, as her father did not consider him a suitable match. However, Drake continued to visit her at Combe Sydenham and managed to persuade her to wait for him until his next return from sea.

It seems that Elizabeth had to wait rather too long for the return of her handsome and dashing suitor, and eventually agreed to marry someone else. On the very day of the wedding, as she was about to enter the church, there was a sudden flash and a large ball fell to the ground at her feet. Elizabeth, convinced that Drake had deliberately fired a cannon-ball from his ship, refused to continue with the ceremony.

Having achieved this remarkable feat, Sir Francis Drake soon arrived himself at Combe Sydenham and he and Elizabeth were married in 1585. Sir Francis died ten years later and Elizabeth then married Sir William Courtenay of Powderham Castle in Devon.

The 'cannon-ball' was kept at Combe Sydenham, as a reminder of this dramatic and romantic event. Later it was identified as a meteorite – but some people will say anything to spoil a good story!

JULIANA HORATIA EWING

1841–1885
(née Gatty)
Buried: All Saints' Churchyard, Trull

Juliana Ewing, highly successful writer of children's stories, died in Bath in May 1885 aged only forty-four. Always delicate, she had been taken ill at her home in Taunton, Somerset, and was buried in the churchyard of her parish church at Trull. There is a window to her memory in the church there.

Juliana was born in Yorkshire and from an early age showed a talent for story-telling. Her mother started a regular journal for children, *Aunt Judy's Magazine*, to which Juliana first contributed a piece called 'Mrs Overtheway's Remembrances'. In 1867 she married Major Alexander Ewing and set off for New Brunswick, where they lived for two years, and then returned to Aldershot in England. Juliana wrote steadily throughout this time and, in 1873, took over joint editorship of *Aunt Judy's Magazine* with her sister. The same year saw the publication of her best-known stories, *Lob-lie-by-the-Fire*.

In 1883, after some years of separation due to her ill-health, Juliana and her husband settled in Taunton and a year later *Jackanapes*, her most popular book, was published. In 1885, suffering from blood-poisoning, she was taken to Bath and died after an operation.

Juliana Ewing's stories were delightful. She never patronized her reader and had a wonderful sense of humour:

Benjy was a bad boy. His name was Benjamin, but he was always called Benjy. He looked like something ending in JY or GY or rather DGY, such as *Podgy*. Indeed he was podgy, and moreover Smudgy, having that cloudy, slovenly look (like a slate *smudged* instead of washed) which is characteristic of people whose morning toilet is not so thorough as it should be. (Juliana Ewing, *Lob-lie-by-the-Fire*, 1873)

MARGERY FISH
1893–1969
(née Townshend)
Lived: East Lambrook Manor, South Petherton

The house was long and low, in the shape of an L, built of honey-coloured Somerset stone. At one time it must have been thatched but, unfortunately, that had been discarded long ago and old red tiles used instead. (Margery Fish, *We Made a Garden*, 1956)

In 1937 Margery and Walter Fish bought East Lambrook Manor, South Petherton, in Somerset. They were about to retire and were looking for a peaceful retreat in the country. East Lambrook was very run down and they almost decided not to take it.

It took years of hard work to restore the house and rescue the garden. Margery, who knew almost nothing about gardening, has since been described as 'the doyen of gardeners'. Her many books about gardening: *We Made a Garden, Cottage Garden Flowers, Ground Cover Plants*, etc. are still very popular and East Lambrook is a byword among garden lovers.

She died in 1969. The garden and the nursery she created remain as her memorial and continue to be open to the public at certain times. (As with any visit of this kind, it is best to find out *before* one goes what the admission times are.)

DION FORTUNE

1891–1946
(née Violet Mary Firth)
Buried: Glastonbury
town cemetery

Those who have seen the famous Glastonbury Tor, about which so many legends gather, are always perplexed as to whether it is natural or artificial. Its pyramidal form, set in the centre of a great plain, is almost too good to be true – too appropriate to be the unaided work of Nature. Viewed from near at hand, a terraced track can clearly be seen winding in three tiers round the cone of the Tor, and this is indisputably the work of man. (Dion Fortune, *Avalon of the Heart*, 1934)

Dion Fortune was a mystic and one of the most interesting figures in twentieth-century occultism. She was also a writer and her studies of the occult tradition, such as *The Mystical Qabalah*, and novels such as *Moon Magic*, and *The Goat-Foot God*, are still in print.

Born Violet Firth, she was the daughter of a Llandudno hotel proprietor. In her early twenties she suffered a nervous breakdown and this probably led to her decision to study psychology. She developed a deep interest in occultism and joined the magical 'Order of the Golden Dawn'. Later she broke away and founded the 'Society of the Inner Light'.

In the 1920s Dion Fortune, as she was now known, moved to Glastonbury and eventually bought a property on the lower slope of Glastonbury Tor. It was here, at Chalice Orchard, that she organized and ran an esoteric hostel. Her writing continued unabated:

She foreshadowed the interests of generations after her. She was ahead of her time, for instance, in raising the issue of female spirituality which American feminists began airing about 1975, in protest against 'patriarchal' religion. (Geoffrey Ashe *Avalonian Quest*, 1982)

Dion Fortune died at Glastonbury in her mid-fifties. She was buried in the town cemetery.

THE FAIR MAIDS OF FOXCOTE

St Philip and St James
Church, Norton St Philip

In a small room under the tower of the Church of St Philip and St James in Norton St Philip, are two stone heads, representing the Fair Maids of Foxcote. Under their impassive faces hangs the copy of a

quotation from the diary of Samuel Pepys, who saw the original tombstone on the floor of the nave in 1668:

At Philip's Norton I walked to the Church, and there saw the tombstone whereon there were only two heads cut, which the story goes and creditably, were two sisters, called the Fair Maids of Foscott [Foxcote – a nearby village], that had two bodies upward and one stomach, and there lie buried.

Nothing seems to be known of the birth, life or death of these very early Siamese twins but, although the heads are blurred and worn by time, it is evident that they were not children when they died.

QUEEN GUINEVERE (GWENHWYFAR)

Glastonbury Abbey Ruins, Glastonbury

In the ruins of the old abbey at Glastonbury stands this notice:

In the year 1191 the bodies of King Arthur and his Queen were said to have been found on the south side of the Lady Chapel. On 19th April 1278 their remains were removed in the presence of King Edward I and Queen Eleanor to a black marble tomb on this site. This tomb survived until the Dissolution of the Abbey in 1539.

Guinevere (the Celtic version is Gwenhwyfar) is also linked with Amesbury in Wiltshire where she is said to have retired to do penance after the King discovered that she had been unfaithful. Arthur is supposed to have visited her there to say goodbye and Guinevere remained at Amesbury until her death:

The corpse . . . was carried by night in a sombre cortège . . . to be laid close to Arthur. On dark nights the spectral flickering of the torches that lit the route for her bier have been seen moving along the road from Shepton Mallet above Glastonbury. (Berta Lawrence, *Somerset Legends*, 1973)

LADY MARGARET HUNGERFORD

c. 1673
(née Holliday)
Hungerford Tomb,
Farleigh Hungerford
Castle

Inside St Anne's Chapel at Farleigh Hungerford Castle is the magnificent tomb of Sir Edward Hungerford and his wife, Margaret. Their figures have been described as 'the best sculptures of Stuart times'.

Lady Margaret Hungerford ordered the tomb when her

husband died in 1648. She was also responsible for the decoration of the Chapel of St Anne and was the founder of the Hungerford Almshouses at Corsham in Wiltshire.

FLORENCE KETTLEWELL

1856–1934
(née Olphert)
Buried: East Harptree
Cemetery

I can claim no qualifications as an author and these jottings are merely a sample record of a happy period in England, amongst the truest and best of friends. (Mrs F. B. Kettlewell, *'Trinkum-Trinkums' of Fifty Years*, 1927)

Florence Kettlewell moved to East Harptree, Somerset (now Avon), when she married William Wildman Kettlewell JP in 1875. She lived at Harptree Court, once the home of Lady Waldegrave (q.v.) and had three sons. After her husband's death in 1916 Mrs Kettlewell moved to Harptree House and, when she was seventy, published a small book called

'Trinkum-Trinkums' of Fifty Years. Packed with legends and local stories, most of them told to her by word of mouth, it is a delightful book and an interesting portrait of village life. The title was inspired by a comment made by one of the villagers:

> Whilst I was engaged in collecting folklore, my old friend, Felix Board, remarked to the Rector one day, 'Can't think what Mrs Kettlewell be up to with her Trinkum-Trinkums'!

Mrs Kettlewell died in 1934 and was buried in the cemetery at East Harptree.

MRS LEAKEY

fl. 1636
Lived: Minehead

Mrs Leakey of Minehead must be one of the most eccentric ghosts in English history. She not only haunted and terrified her own family, she also specialized in whistling up storms at sea.

In his notes to *Rokeby*, a poem about the Civil War, Sir Walter Scott told Mrs Leakey's story so well that it is unnecessary to do more than quote him:

> The most formidable whistler that I remember to have met with was the apparition of a certain Mrs Leakey, who about 1636 resided, as we are told, at Mynehead, in Somerset, where her only son drove a considerable trade between that port and Waterford, and was the owner of several vessels. This old gentlewoman was of a social disposition, and so acceptable to her friends that they used to say to her and to each other, it were a pity such an excellent, good-natured old lady should die; to which she was wont to reply, that whatever pleasure they might find in her company just now, they would

not greatly like to see or converse with her after death . . .
Accordingly, after her death and funeral, she began to appear to various persons by night and by noon-day, in her own house, in the town and fields, at sea and upon shore. So far had she departed from her former urbanity, that she is recorded to have kicked a doctor of medicine for his impolite negligence in omitting to hand her over a stile. It was also her humour to appear upon the quay, and call for a boat. But especially so soon as any of her son's ships approached the harbour, this ghost would appear in the same garb and likeness as when she was alive, and standing at the mainmast, would blow with a whistle, and though it were never so great a calm, yet immediately there would arise a most dreadful storm, that would break, wreck and drown ship and goods. When she had thus proceeded until her son had neither credit to freight a vessel, nor could have procured men to sail in it, she began to attack the persons of his family, and actually strangled their only child in the cradle.

etail of the Hungerford tomb at Farleigh Hungerford Castle

St Michael and All Angels Church, Bawdrip

ELEANOR LOVELL

d. 1681
St Michael and All Angels
Church, Bawdrip

The mistletoe hung in the castle hall,
The holly branch shone on the old
  oak wall;
And the Baron's retainers were blythe
  and gay,
And keeping their Christmas holiday.
The Baron beheld with a father's
  Pride,
His beautiful child, young Lovell's
  Bride;
While she, with her bright eyes
  seemed to be,
The star of the goodly company.

In 1840 Thomas Haynes Bayly's
popular narrative poem, *The
Mistletoe Bough*, was published.
Although he used poetic licence
and changed the background, the
story itself is supposed to have
been inspired by a terrible event
that took place in Somerset one
hundred and fifty-nine years
previously.
   In the old church at Bawdrip,
Somerset (unfortunately hidden
behind the altar) there is a tablet
recording the tragic death of
Eleanor Lovell. She was the

rector's, not the baron's, 'beautiful
child', and was married in this very
church. During the celebrations
after the wedding, a game of hide
and seek was suggested and
Eleanor was the first to hide.

They sought her that night, and they
  sought her next day,
And they sought her in vain when a
  week passed away.

Eleanor had hidden too well, and
the place she had chosen was not
discovered for many years:

At length an old chest that had long
  lain hid,
Was found in the castle . . . they
  raised the lid . . .
And a skeleton form lay mouldering
  there,
In the bridal wreath of that lady fair.
Oh, sad was her fate! . . . in sportive
  jest,
She hid from her lord in the old oak
  chest . . .
It closed with a spring! . . . and
  dreadful doom,
The bride lay clasp'd in her living
  tomb.

JANE LOW

1834?–1913
(née Hooper)
Plaque: St Laurence
Church, East Harptree

Another cause for praise is the
merciful preservation of comparative
health during the wave of heat which
passed over Palestine in August. For
sixteen days the temperature was
fiery, and not a breath of air stirred to
mitigate it. (Mrs J. Low, 'Annual
Letters of the Missionaries', 1896)

There is a tendency, even now, to
believe that Englishwomen in the
eighteen-hundreds were all fragile,
over-protected and subject to
vapours. For the majority this may
have been true, but there were still
thousands who managed to break
the mould and among them were
the missionaries. Some, like
Mildred Cable (q.v.), were
exceptional and became famous.
Others laboured in India, Africa,
Palestine and China, but have been
almost entirely forgotten.
   In 1861 Jane Hooper of
Somerset left England to join her
brother in India. She took charge
of the Female Normal School at
Benares and learned Hindi and
Urdu. In 1864 she married
Lieutenant Low, insisting that the
ceremony be held in Hindustani, so

that her pupils could understand
the service. She gave birth to two
daughters one of whom died of
heat stroke. Then her husband was
invalided out of the army and they
returned to England.
   In 1875, Jane and her daughter
arrived at the mission in Palestine.
She began to learn Arabic and
spent the rest of her life – mainly at
Kefr-Yasif – teaching and working
for the Church Missionary Society.
It was hard and sometimes disappointing work. Jane once wrote:

The greater part of the peasant
  women work all through the week,
  even harder than the men. Only a few
  can spare the time to come to the
  Thursday afternoon meeting, and
  when they do come they are often too
  tired and go fast to sleep.

In 1897 Jane retired but
continued to live in Palestine.
When she died she was buried in
the Protestant cemetery in
Jerusalem. Her daughter placed a
plaque in East Harptree Church,
Somerset, to the memory of her
dedicated, independent and
hard-working mother.

DOROTHY ANN SHELMADINE LOWE

1880–1976
Lived: Hinton St George

Miss D. Lowe, J.P., a former chairman of County Executive, gained an M.B.E. for her hospital work in the First War. In World War II she was awarded the Greek Order of Chevalier of St George for her work among the Greek villages. Owing to her enthusiasm and hard work, about £1,000 was subscribed by Somerset . . . for schools, ambulances and the restoration of a water supply, to Kalavryta. Miss Lowe's talks in Greek costume on her experiences in Greece delighted many W.I. audiences. (*The Somerset Women's Institutes' Golden Jubilee Book*, 1965)

Dorothy Lowe was born in Lancashire but moved with her parents to West Coker, Somerset, when she was eighteen. Four years later they moved again, this time only as far as Hinton St George. Hinton was to be Dorothy's home for the rest of her life. She became Commandant of the Hinton Red Cross in 1911 and head of the hospital in Hinton House from 1914 to 1918. When the First World War was over, she promptly founded the Hinton Women's Institute and in 1927 joined the National Committee of the WI.

Her love of travel, and particularly her love of Greece, led to her becoming secretary of the Somerset Committee formed for the adoption of devastated Greek villages after the Second World War. Hinton St George owes its village hall and playing fields to her persistence, and, as well as an MBE and a Belgian decoration, she was awarded the Freedom of Kalavryta in Greece. When she was eighty-eight she joined the fiftieth birthday party celebrations of the WI, which included a visit to the bulb fields in Holland. She died aged ninety-five and was buried at Hinton.

KATHARINE MALTWOOD

d. 1961
The Temple of the Stars, best seen from the summit of Glastonbury Tor

King Arthur's Round Table was not just a piece of furniture as might be supposed but something vastly more worthy upon which to found a Knightly Order; his table was the Round Table of the Stars . . . This design was found laid out on the ground near Glastonbury, and is 30 miles in circumference, the earthworks which form it were constructed by the early Bronze Age inhabitants; it constitutes a sculptural relief of unequalled magnitude.

After this confident statement in her book, *The Enchantments of Britain* (1944), Katharine Maltwood proceeds, with the help of maps, models and literary clues, to give precise directions to and detailed descriptions of giant figures representing the zodiac: 'The Scorpion, Archer, Goat, Water-Carrier, Fishes, Young Ram, Bull, Twins, Lion and Virgin'.

Katharine, the daughter of a judge, studied at the Slade School of Art. In the 1920s she began her illustrations for 'The High History of the Holy Grail', a thirteenth-century Norman manuscript:

> When deep in the text of the book she realised that there was a relationship between the ground plan it described in and around Glastonbury and the ancient constellation zodiac in the heavens. (M. Mathias and D. Hector, *Glastonbury*, 1979)

Utterly convinced that she had discovered the largest of Britain's antiquities, Katharine wrote *A Guide to Glastonbury's Temple of the Stars* (1935) followed by *The Enchantments of Britain*: 'I lay claim to the discovery, delineation and localization of these effigy constellation giants.'

She did not receive the academic recognition she had hoped for and died in Vancouver, Canada, leaving a large bequest for the furtherance of archaeological research in Somerset.

Opposite: **The Temple of the Stars**

HELEN MATHERS (MRS REEVES)

1853–1920
(née Mathews)
Lived: Misterton

The colour of her hair was Helen Mathers's greatest trouble in her childhood. It was a rich red, and in the familiar home circle she was called 'Carrots', to her great annoyance, until she was sixteen. She says: 'It gave me such genuine distress that before I was nine years old, I had written a story depicting the sufferings of a red-haired girl who wanted to marry a man who was in love with her golden-haired sister. I inscribed this in an old pocket-book, looking out the names and places in the *Times* each day, and afterwards, in agonies of shyness, I read it aloud to the assembled family, who received it with shouts of mirth! (Helen Black, *Notable Women Authors of the Day*, 1906)

Helen Mathews, using the pseudonym Mathers, wrote twenty novels, among them the immensely successful *Comin' Thro' the Rye*, published in three volumes in 1875. Born at Misterton in Somerset, she was brought up there and educated at Chantry School, Frome. In 1875, already

established as a popular writer, she married Dr Henry Reeves, a surgeon, and moved to London. Her novels were always romantic and quite often tragic – almost guaranteeing a 'good cry' – but were rescued from the pitfall of mere sentimentality by a light touch and a dry sense of humour. *Comin' Thro' the Rye*, perhaps the saddest of Helen Mathers's stories, opens with the children of a family exchanging some amusing epitaphs that they have been collecting:

'Poor Martha Snell, her's gone away;
Her would if her could, but her couldn't stay;
Her'd two sore legs and a baddish cough,
But her legs it was as carried her off.'

Hardly anyone nowadays has heard of Helen Mathers or *Comin' Thro' the Rye* which, at the time, was published in several languages – including Sanskrit.

EVELEEN PERKINS

1867–1946?
Wells Museum

The small, but very interesting museum near the cathedral at Wells, has a collection of about one hundred samplers. A few of these are examples of late eighteenth-century and children's work, but the majority were made by Miss Eveleen Perkins of Wells. Eveleen died in the 1940s and her sister, Hilda, gave them to the museum. They have been on display there since 1956.

MARGARET POLE, COUNTESS OF SALISBURY

1473–1541
(née Plantagenet)
Born: Farleigh Hungerford Castle, Farleigh Hungerford

Margaret was born in Somerset, at Farleigh Castle. Her father was George, Duke of Clarence, her uncle Richard III.

She was married to Sir Richard Pole in about 1491 and gave birth to four sons and one daughter. Her husband died in 1505, leaving her with estates in the West Country, Hampshire and Essex.

During the reign of Henry VIII, Margaret was put in charge of his eldest daughter, Princess Mary (child of his first wife, Catherine of Aragon), but when Henry divorced Catherine and married Anne Boleyn, Margaret Pole found herself in an ambiguous situation. Her position was hardly improved

by the fact that her family were not only all devout Catholics, but one of her sons, Cardinal Reginald Pole, had offended Henry VIII deeply when he published his *Pro Ecclesiastione Unitatis Defensione* in 1536.

In 1538 Henry VIII moved against the family. Cardinal Pole was in Italy but two other sons were arrested and later executed. Margaret herself was questioned closely at her home in Hampshire. Her goods were then seized and she was moved away from her home. In 1539 she was taken to the Tower of London and accused of treason; two years later she was executed. The executioner was a novice, who bungled his duty horrifically, hacking clumsily at her neck and shoulders, before he succeeded in cutting off her head. Margaret Pole was sixty-seven when she died. Her property, including her manor of Somerton, in Somerset, was seized by the King. Years later it was granted to the Earl of Huntingdon (who had married Margaret's granddaughter) by Mary Tudor.

ELIZABETH ROWE

**1674–1737
(née Singer)**
Plaque: Rook Lane House, Christchurch Street, Frome

Mrs Rowe was of a moderate stature, her hair of a fine auburn colour, and her eyes of a darkish grey, inclining to blue, and full of fire. Her complexion was very fair and a natural rosy blush glowed in her cheeks. She spoke gracefully, and her voice was exceeding sweet and harmonious. (Jackson's *Library of Christian Biography*, 1837)

Born at Ilchester in Somerset, Elizabeth was the daughter of a Nonconformist minister. She showed an unusual interest in the arts from an early age and, when she was twenty-two, published *Poems on Several Occasions by Philomela*. Her work was admired by the poet, Matthew Prior and praised by Dr Isaac Watts, the hymn-writer.

In 1709, aged thirty-five, Elizabeth met a young writer called Thomas Rowe in Bath – he was twenty-two. They were married the following year and moved to London, but five years later Thomas died of consumption and Elizabeth, deeply shocked and unhappy, returned to Somerset and settled in Frome. She continued to write and, in 1728, published

Friendship in Death, in Twenty Letters from the Dead to the Living. She died at Frome and was buried at the Meeting House there. In 1974 the Frome Society for Local Study placed a plaque on her house in Christchurch Street.

Elizabeth Rowe's *Friendship in Death*, a mixture of poetry and prose, is a moving attempt to understand the agony of the human condition:

> The drift of these letters is, to impress the notion of the soul's immortality; without which, all virtue and all religion with their temporal and eternal good consequences, must fall to the ground.

To do this she composed letters from those who had died, such as 'To the Countess of ——, from her only Son, who died when he was two years old', and 'To my Lord ——, from his deceased wife'. When she ran out of contemporary examples, she used historical, classical and romantic figures to illustrate her own loss and her belief in the possibility of religious and spiritual recovery.

Old Meeting House, Frome where Elizabeth Rowe was buried

DOROTHY WADHAM

1534–1618
(Née Petre)
Buried: Wadham Chapel,
The Minster, Ilminster

Dorothy Petre married Nicholas Wadham in 1555. Her husband's dearest wish was to found a college at Oxford and at their home in Ilton, Somerset, he spent much of his life making plans and drawing up statutes. However, when he died in 1609, the college was still only a dream.

Dorothy Wadham buried her husband, rolled up her sleeves, purchased a suitable site in Oxford, and got down to the practicalities of life. Work on the building began and, four years later, in 1613, Wadham College was built.

Dorothy was an extremely generous woman. Although strongly attracted to the 'old' (Roman Catholic) religion, she loyally made sure that the college was founded in conformity to the Established (Protestant) Church – as her husband would have wished. Before she died, she had an epitaph inscribed in Latin on his tomb:

He still shines. Do you not see? Look at the towers set on the other side of the Isis. What habitations he built for the Muses, what temples for gods!

Dorothy Wadham helped to make some amendments to the College Statutes in its early years, and took a great interest in its development until her death in 1618. She was buried with her husband in the Wadham Chapel in the Minster at Ilminster.

FRANCES, COUNTESS WALDEGRAVE

1821–1879
(Née Braham)
Memorial: St Mary
Magdalene Church,
Chewton Mendip

Lady Waldegrave became one of the most famous society hostesses in London. Her house there was a favourite meeting place for politicians and an invitation to Carlton Gardens, Strawberry Hill or Chewton Priory in Somerset was much sought after.

The daughter of a flamboyant opera singer, John Braham, Frances married four times. Her first husband died within a year of their marriage. Very soon after this she married his brother, George, seventh Earl Waldegrave, and was introduced to Harptree Court, his house in Somerset:

The arrival at Harptree Court was a tremendous affair. All the tenants turned out, triumphal arches appeared overnight, Waldegrave's yeomanry were there in force, and at the top of the beautiful tower of

Chewton Mendip Church a man with a telescope was stationed to warn the bell-ringers both at Chewton and East Harptree, of the carriage's approach. (Wyndham Hewett, *Strawberry Fair*, 1956)

When Lord Waldegrave died in 1846, Frances inherited the whole of the Waldegrave estates and just over a year later married George Granville Harcourt of Nuneham. Her fourth and final marriage, in 1863, was to Chichester Fortescue, Lord Carlingford.

Although most of her time was spent in London, Frances visited Somerset regularly and often entertained at Chewton Priory (having sold Harptree Court). When she died she was buried in the churchyard at Chewton Mendip.

THE WITCH OF WOOKEY

Wookey Hole

In anciente days tradition showes
A base and wicked elfe arose –
The Witch of Wokey hight;
No wholesome herb could here be found,
She blasted every plant around
And blister'd every flock.
(Henry Harrington, *The Witch of Wokey*, 1756)

An old witch is said to have lived in Wookey Hole by herself. She so terrorized the inhabitants of Wookey that they begged for help from the Church. A monk was sent from Glastonbury to carry out the exorcism and finally, when everything else had failed, he

Memorial to Frances, Countess Waldegrave in St Mary Magdalene Church, Chewton Mendip

scooped up water from the lake inside the cave, blessed it and threw it at her. She instantly turned to stone.

When Herbert Balch, the archaeologist, excavated the Great Cave (1904–1915), he discovered evidence of human habitation dating from 250 BC. Some bones that he found, once thought to be those of the witch, are probably the remains of a goatherd. They are now in the museum at Wells.

Brass of Florence Wyndham, in St Decuman's Church, Watchet

FLORENCE WYNDHAM

d. 1596
(née Wadham)
Buried: St Decuman's
Church, Watchet

Florence Wyndham is buried in St Decuman's church, Watchet, in Somerset, and a brass there shows her chatting to her husband. Her story, if it is true, is a bizarre one.

The Wyndham family owned both Orchard Wyndham and Kentisford Farm. Florence, the wife of Sir John Wyndham, had only been married for two years when she fell ill and died. She was buried in the family vault in the church close to her home at Kentisford.

In those days, this was a tragic but unexceptional event and the family returned home to mourn the loss, totally unprepared for what was about to take place.

It seems that the night following the funeral, the verger, who had attended the ceremony, returned secretly to steal some of the jewellery that had been left on Florence's body. While he was attempting to remove a ring, to his unutterable horror the 'corpse' sat up and began to speak! Understandably he fled – and was never seen again.

Florence Wyndham, with her shroud fluttering around her, stumbled out of the church and made her way home, where she knocked on the door. The terror of the servant who answered this summons can well be imagined, and it took a little while before her husband was convinced that *he* was not seeing a ghost.

Florence recovered fairly quickly from her ordeal and, not long afterwards, gave birth to a son. She lived to a ripe old age before being buried (for the second time!) in St Decuman's church.

WILTSHIRE

MARY-CAROLINE, MARCHIONESS OF AILESBURY
d. 1892
(née Herbert)
Memorial: St Katharine's Church, Savernake

The second Marchioness of Ailesbury, Lady Brudenell-Bruce, lived at Tottenham House, near Marlborough. Her husband, the Marquis, was Warden of the Forest of Savernake.

Mary-Caroline was a strong-minded woman of high principles, who persuaded her husband to build schools for local children. She also founded a training school for girls at Durley, where they could learn a wide variety of domestic skills. In his book, *The Wardens of Savernake Forest* (1949) the Earl of Cardigan described yet another of her achievements:

Perhaps the best known work . . . of this charitable Marchioness was the founding of Savernake Hospital, now a valuable medical centre, serving a large area of Wiltshire. She had it built and endowed as a Cottage Hospital, mainly for the benefit of poor people in the Savernake neighbourhood . . . It soon proved its usefulness – and so has grown to a size and importance beyond what she can have foreseen.

When she died, a memorial to Mary-Caroline was erected in St Katharine's church, on the family estate.

LADY BLANCHE ARUNDELL
1583–1649
(née Somerset)
Buried: St John the Baptist Church, Tisbury

The Civil War, which began in 1642 and for four bitter years divided the nation between King and Parliament, produced heroines as well as heroes. Lady Blanche Arundell became a Royalist heroine when, aged sixty, she bravely defended her home, Wardour Castle in Wiltshire.

In May 1643, a Parliamentary force arrived at the castle. Lady Blanche's husband, Thomas, second Lord Arundell of Wardour, was dying at Oxford of wounds received during a battle. Summoned to surrender, Lady Blanche replied that her husband expected her to keep his home and that she would obey him and no one else. This was a brave piece of defiance, as there were well over a thousand men outside the gates and apart from women and children, only twenty-five inside.

Lady Blanche's tiny garrison held out for just over a week. Women loaded muskets to give the men some rest, and their resistance was only finally broken when mines were detonated beneath the castle walls.

So-called honourable terms were drawn up and agreed, but were promptly and savagely broken by the Parliamentarians. An estimated one hundred thousand pounds of damage was done and Lady Blanche withdrew with little left except her dignity and pride. A year later her son Henry reoccupied Wardour Castle and blew it up to prevent it falling into Parliamentary hands for good.

Lady Blanche lived for some years in Salisbury. She died at Winchester but was buried in the lovely old church at Tisbury, not far from the ruins of her home.

One of the Arundell coat of arms in Tisbury Church

MOTHER BARNES

fl. 1575
Littlecote House, near
Chilton Foliat

One of the most powerful stories to emerge from Wiltshire's past concerns Littlecote House near Chilton Foliat, the owner, William Darrell and an unknown midwife from Berkshire, known as Mother Barnes.

In 1575 Mrs Barnes was awakened late one night by a loud knocking at her door. This was not an unusual event for a midwife, and she went to see who it was. Two complete strangers stood there. They asked her to attend a confinement and offered her a rich reward for doing so. Mother Barnes agreed and prepared to leave with them, managing to quell her fears when they insisted on blindfolding her. The journey seemed to be an unusually long one.

On their arrival at the unknown destination, Mother Barnes, her blindfold removed, found herself in a large house. She recognized no one, and was taken upstairs to a room where a woman was in the last stages of childbirth. Forgetting her doubts, the midwife got down to work and delivered a baby boy. Uncertain as to who she should approach next, she carried the baby into a room nearby and found a man there, standing by a blazing fire. To her horror, when she asked him for something to wrap the baby in, he told her to throw the child into the fire. Mother Barnes begged for its life and even said she would take it home and bring it up as her own, but she was ignored. The baby was taken from her and burnt to death. Some time later, Mother Barnes was taken home – blindfolded as before.

Years later, William or 'Wild' Darrell, as he was known, of Littlecote House, was formally accused of murder. Mother Barnes was involved once again. It seems that while she was there on that dreadful night she had cut a piece off the bedcover, and this piece of material had identified the scene of the crime. The case dragged on for years; Wild Darrell had relations in high places and eventually nothing was proved.

The story, believed by many, was that while a neighbour, Sir Henry Knyvett, was away, Darrell had an affair with Lady Knyvett and had made her pregnant. Sir Henry was a wealthy and influential neighbour and Darrell, deciding to conceal the evidence, sent for Mother Barnes. When Darrell died, fourteen years later, his cousin (and legal adviser), Sir John Popham, inherited Littlecote House.

Not surprisingly, a landing on the first floor is supposed to be haunted. Mother Barnes is also said to have put a curse on the Pophams: no first-born son of theirs would survive to inherit

Littlecote House

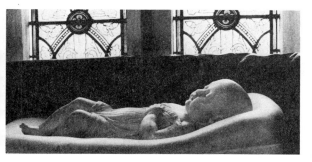

Littlecote House. In the church of Chilton Foliat nearby there is a pathetic sculpture of a small baby. It is a memorial to Francis Hugh Leybourne-Popham who died, aged five months, in 1861. He was, it is said, the last of the first-born sons of the Popham family.

Memorial to Francis Hugh Leybourne-Popham in Chilton Foliat Church

---

ANN BEACH

c. 1740
Lived: Old Manor House, Keevil

Keevil in Wiltshire is a very beautiful village and it is certainly worth stopping there for a short visit.

Opposite the church, behind a high wall, stands the Old Manor House (privately owned and *not* open to visitors), which was once the home of the Squire of Keevil and his only daughter and heiress, Ann.

Ann fell in love with the local curate. Her father refused to allow them to marry and shut her away in a room above the porch. She was kept there for two long years and, during her imprisonment, she scratched this brief, helpless

message on the window pane:

Remember Ann Beach 1740

Throughout the two years, Ann consistently refused to change her mind and, on her release, her father allowed the marriage to take place. He then cut her out of his will, and there perhaps lies the real tragedy. Ann's new husband, the curate, had, after all, only been interested in her money and when he realized he had lost that, he also lost all interest in Ann. It is said that he treated her so badly that she died only a year after her marriage.

MARGARET SARAH CARPENTER

1793–1872
(née Geddes)
Born: Salisbury

It cannot be denied that since the days of Angelica Kauffman and Mary Moser, and the female honorary members of the same period, the Academy has studiously ignored the existence of women artists, leaving them to work in the cold shade of utter neglect.

These severe words were written by Ellen Clayton in her *English Female Artists* (1876) and they were written on behalf of Margaret Carpenter.

Margaret was born at Salisbury, Wiltshire, and showed an unusual ability in art from an early age. At first she was tutored in figure-drawing and painting by a local teacher; later Lord Radnor gave her permission to copy in his gallery at Longford Castle. It was Lord Radnor who also encouraged her to send some of her work to the

Society of Arts and in 1814 advised her to London herself.

Margaret soon established herself there as a portrait painter and, during her first year, exhibited a portrait of Lord Folkestone at the Academy and a painting called *The Fortune Teller* at the British Institution. Three years later she married William Carpenter, who became Keeper of Prints and Drawings at the British Museum. She had several children but continued to paint and exhibit her work.

When her husband died Margaret Carpenter was granted a pension of one hundred pounds a year, which was intended as a recognition of her own merit as well as an acknowledgement of her husband's services. She died in London, aged eighty.

MARY CHANDLER

1687–1745
Born: Malmesbury

Mary Chandler was born at
Malmesbury in Wiltshire. With
very little prospect of marriage –
she was born with a deformed
spine and her health was poor –
she moved to Bath as a young
woman, and set up as a shopkeeper
there. Her hobby was poetry. She
wrote rhyming riddles and poems
for her friends who enjoyed them
so much that they eventually
persuaded her to publish. In 1736
a volume of her poetry, *The
Description of Bath*, appeared.
Then, suddenly and quite
unexpectedly, romance entered
Mary Chandler's life.

An elderly gentleman walked
into her shop one day. He said he
had come a long way to visit her
and had read and much admired
her poetry. He bought a pair of
gloves and then proposed
marriage. Mary, considerably
shaken and more than a little
tempted, decided to refuse the offer
and her admirer, with great
dignity, departed.

When a sixth edition of Mary's
book was published in 1744, it
included a new poem called *A True
Tale*. In it, Mary describes her
feelings over the incident, and the
reasons for her decision. She asks
us to laugh at her, but not her 'little
man'.

> For he was very good, and clean,
>   and civil;
> And tho's his Taste was *odd*, you
>   own, not *evil* . . .

I never in my Life was half so scar'd
Fourscore long Miles, to buy a
    crooked Wife!

After he has made his proposal
she retires, covered with
confusion:

> Much more he spake, but I have half
>   forgot;
> I went to Bed, but could not sleep a
>   *Jot*.
> A Thing so Unexpected! and so
>   New! . . .
> I own, it made me pause for half that
>   Night;
> Then wak'd, and soon recover'd
>   from my fright;
> Resolv'd, and put an End to the
>   Affair;
> So great a Change, this late, I could
>   not bear.

Mary had lived alone too long
and was unwilling to give up her
independence:

> And, when I will, I ramble, or retire
> To my own Room, own Bed, my
>   Garden, Fire;
> Take up my Book, or trifle with my
>   Pen;
> And, when I'm weary, lay them down
>   again:
> No Questions ask'd.

Somewhere, one hopes, Mary's
'little man' read her graceful
explanation and was comforted by
her final words: -

> And thus this whole Affair begins
>   and ends:
> We met as *Lovers*, and we parted
>   Friends.

MAUD EDITH CUNNINGTON

1869–1951
(née Pegge)
Lived: 33 Long Street,
Devizes

Maud Cunnington and her
husband Benjamin were both
archaeologists. They lived in
Wiltshire and excavated several
sites there, including Woodhenge.

Maud became particularly
interested in the monuments of
Avebury parish, which include two
stone avenues, the tallest artificial
hill in Europe (Silbury), and the
largest prehistoric tomb in England
(West Kennet). A neolithic site,
mentioned in the past and thought
to be on Overton Hill, had not
been traced. Maud was struck by a

chance remark of William
Stukeley, the eighteenth century
antiquarian, who mentioned that
one could see something called 'the
serpent's head' on Overton Down,
if one stood near Fox's Covert,
west of Beckhampton:

> Mrs Cunnington placed herself at the
> crucial spot, and then she found that
> there was only one point in the
> millfield which could be seen from
> there. But how to identify this, after
> walking from one place to the other?
> A bright idea came to her. She
> counted the telegraph posts between

the two positions. This seemed to promise to be more explicit, and indeed it was; for on the exact spot which the telegraph posts indicated they excavated and found the holes in which the two circles of stones had originally stood. (Edith Olivier, *Wiltshire*, 1951)

Maud Cunnington had discovered the site now known as the Sanctuary.

Her publications include those on the Sanctuary itself, Woodhenge, Casterley Camp and *Avebury: A guide to the Circles, the Church, the Manor House* (1931). She was awarded the CBE in 1948, was an Honorary Life Member of the Cambrian Archaeological Association and the Society of Antiquaries, Scotland, and was the first woman president of the Wiltshire Archaeological and Natural History Society.

Avebury village

143

DIANA DORS

1931–1984
(née Fluck)
Born: Swindon

I'm not for Women's Lib, but it *is* a man's world, and I've had to behave like a man because I've been up against them. I've been shaped by them, guided by them and manipulated by them. Yes, that's it, *man*-ipulated; maybe it's just that I've never never been wronged by women . . . Sometimes I think we should throw in the towel and go for the little thatched cottage in Wiltshire, that's where I'm from and I love it. (Diana Dors, interviewed for *The Sunday Times*, 1982)

Diana Dors, who died of cancer in 1984, was born at Swindon in Wiltshire, the daughter of an army captain, Peter Fluck, and his wife Mary. She took elocution lessons when she was only six and in her teens attended classes at the Tanwood School of Dancing, Swindon.

In 1946 Diana became a student at the London Academy of Music and Dramatic Art (LAMDA), and then joined the Rank Charm School for Starlets. She was offered a part in the film, *The Shop at Sly Corner*, when she was still only fourteen years old, and changed her surname from Fluck to Dors.

From that time onwards, the career of Diana Dors became, as *The Times* headlined her obituary in 1984, 'Conspicuous . . . on and off the screen'. She appeared briefly in *Oliver Twist*, worked for Sir Carol Reed in *A Kid for Two*

Diana Dors

Farthings and in 1956 made a deliberate attempt to be taken seriously in the film *Yield to the Night*.

Diana Dors married three times. Separated from her first husband, Dennis Hamilton, in 1957, she then married Dickie Dawson, an American comedian, and gave birth to two sons. In 1968 she married the actor, Alan Lake, and the same year was declared bankrupt. A brave and determined woman, she struggled through years of neglect, scandal and criticism, gave birth to a third son, published her memoirs and, in 1974, played Queen Jocasta at The Chichester Festival.

In the 1980s, Diana Dors launched herself on a new career writing an agony column in a daily newspaper and appearing on breakfast television in a slimming feature.

She died in 1984 aged only fifty-two.

MARY ALICE DOUGLAS
d. 1941
The Godolphin School, Salisbury

We have all valued and profited by her quick decision and unerring detection of any weak spot in a plan, or flaw in an argument. What an inspiration it has been to work under one so unfailingly courteous and chivalrously considerate! Her love of all beauty is shown in every part of the fabric of the school, and her greatest joy has been to make it the happy place it is. (A. E. Awdry, *Miss Douglas – An Appreciation*, Godolphin School Magazine, 1919)

The daughter of Canon Douglas of Salwarpe, Worcestershire, Mary Alice went to Lincoln Training College and then Westfield College. She was second mistress at a school in Worcester for eight years and, in 1889, was appointed headmistress of Godolphin School for Girls in Salisbury, Wiltshire. When she took up office there were 22 girls at the school; when she resigned in 1919 there were 230. She had worked for thirty years to build the school up into one of the best in the country:

Fifty years ago girls' schools were governed by a set of rigid rules, but from the first Miss Douglas struck the note of freedom, freedom for both staff and girls. Discipline she expected, but it was self-discipline, voluntarily accepted out of consideration for others, its keynote courtesy, its aim the general well-being. (*The Times*, 1941)

MAISIE GAY
1883–1945
(née Daisy Munro-Noble)
Lived: Box

Being what Americans call homely, I am a non-starter in the beauty stakes. Besides I have no illusions about myself, and all my life I have had to sharpen my wits, keep my brain well dusted, and rely on what intelligence the good Lord gave me to pull me through. (Maisie Gay, *Laughing Through Life*, 1931)

The much-loved musical comedy, revue and music-hall star, Maisie Gay, made her last appearance on stage in 1932. She retired to Box, in Wiltshire, and died there in 1945, having spent the previous ten years confined to her bed.

Born Daisy Munro-Noble she was educated both in Germany and at the North London Collegiate School for Girls. She took singing lessons and her first part was in a play called *The Cherry Girl*. She changed her name to Maisie Gay, worked at the old Gaiety Theatre in London and then, in 1911, appeared in America as Madame Blum in *The Quaker Girl*, followed by a part in *High Jinks*.

Returning home, Maisie worked with Noël Coward in his revue, *London Calling*. In 1930 she began a career in films, with Edgar Wallace's *To Oblige a Lady* but, two years later, ill health forced her to retire from the world of the theatre. In 1941 she made a series of broadcast talks to invalids from her home in Wiltshire.

ELIZABETH GODOLPHIN

1663–1726
(née Godolphin)
Godolphin School,
Salisbury

The Godolphin School in Salisbury owes its existence to Elizabeth, the daughter of Francis Godolphin of Coulston, Wiltshire.

Elizabeth married her second cousin once removed, Charles Godolphin, and, although they were both involved in the founding of a school, 'for the education of eight young orphan gentlewomen in the City of New Sarum', it was Elizabeth who set forth the bequest in her will. She signed the will in June, 1726, just before her death.

LOUISE FRANÇOISE GOUT

1737–1811
(née Pernet)
St Andrew's Church,
Great Durnford

In the nineteenth century, governesses were often considered to be rather inferior members of the household. In the eighteenth century, however, they were sometimes treated not only with respect but with affection.

St Andrew's church at Great Durnford, Wiltshire, has a memorial to the governess of the Harris children of 'the adjoining Manor House'. It was placed there by the Honourable Katherine Robinson and her sister, Louisa Harris, to commemorate Mrs Gout:

who was chosen by their parents to superintend their education in the early part of their lives.

Louise Françoise Pernet came from Paudet, near Lausanne, in the Pays de Vaud, Switzerland. She stayed with the Harris family for over fifty years and, during that time, married and became Mrs Gout. When she died, the two sisters she had taught left their tribute to her with these words:

From the careful manner in which she executed this trust Mrs Gout was considered by them and their family . . . as a most faithful and affectionate friend and for this reason as well as from her unaffected piety and the strict integrity of her character truly deserving of this mark of their esteem and regard.

MAUD HEATH

d. 1474
Statue: Wick Hill, near
Bremhill

Maud Heath's statue was not particularly easy to find. We drove from Lacock (near Chippenham in Wiltshire) and, having come off the main road and negotiated some narrow country lanes, we reached Bremhill. There, we had to ask the way but five minutes later we opened a gate and were standing in a field, gazing at our quarry. There, in the middle of nowhere, was a miniature Nelson's Column, on top of which perched the figure of Maud Heath. She had a stick in one hand, a basket by her side, a bonnet on her head, and was gazing out over the countryside of Wiltshire below.

Maud lived at Langley Burrel and, for much of her life, she walked four miles to Chippenham every week to sell her produce at the market, and then walked home again. This journey was not at all out of the ordinary in those days, but Maud objected to the fact that most of the time her feet were soaking wet by the time she got home.

When she died, she left enough money – eight pounds a year – to maintain a footpath between Wick Hill and Chippenham Clift, so that neighbours, friends and future generations could walk to market in relative comfort. Her footpath, known as Maud Heath's Causeway, still exists over five hundred years later.

In 1838 Henry, Marquis of Lansdowne, Lord of the Manor, and William Bowles, vicar of Bremhill, erected the statue of Maud at their own expense. William Bowles also translated the couplets that were carved in Latin at each end of the Causeway. The one where she began her journey reads:

From this Wick Hill begins the praise
Of Maud Heath's gifts to these
highways.

atue of Maud Heath at Wick Hill, near Bremhill

FORTITUDE
✠ IN MEMORY OF ✠
EDITH MAUD
HULSE
great Lady in deed and

**Memorial to Edith Hulse
in Salisbury Cathedral**

FRANCES, COUNTESS OF HERTFORD AND DUCHESS OF SOMERSET

1699–1754?
(née Thynne)
Marlborough College, Marlborough

Poor stream! held captive by the Frost
Thy current numb'd, thy brightness lost;
Compell'd thy journey to delay,
And on these desert shores to stay,
Thy fortune is to mine ally'd,
Both by superior force are ty'd;
Different captivitys we prove,
Thou bound by cold, and I by love.
(Frances, Countess of Hertford,
Verses Occasion'd by Seeing the River Kennet Frozen Over)

Lady Hertford wrote poetry simply because she enjoyed it. She did not consider her own efforts of any great significance, although she was a friend and patroness of poets.

Married at the age of sixteen to the Earl of Hertford, she developed into a warm, lively, highly intelligent woman, interested in everything that happened around her. She greatly respected Dr Isaac Watts, the popular Nonconformist preacher, and became an enthusiastic supporter of the Methodists.

Lady Hertford spent a great deal of time at the mansion they called Marlborough Castle in Wiltshire and designed a grotto in the grounds there. She had two children, a daughter Elizabeth, and a son George Seymour (Lord Beauchamp). It was to her son that she wrote some of her most natural and charming letters, while he was travelling in Europe:

Saturday Good morrow, my dear Beauchamp, though I have been up these five hours, for I rose at seven, and before nine had wrote part of your letter into my book, walked round the Park, made a cream cheese, and sent to Mr Tash for a warrant to bring a man before him who shot nine of our pigeons.

Eventually the Countess of Hertford's home at Marlborough became a famous coaching-inn, and later still was the first building used for Marlborough College, when it was founded in 1843.

EDITH MAUD HULSE

1866–1937
(née Lawson)
Memorial: Salisbury Cathedral

One of the memorials in Salisbury Cathedral is dedicated to Edith Maud Hulse, who was elected Mayor of Salisbury in 1927: 'A Great Lady', states the inscription, 'in deed and word'. She was delighted to be the first woman in Salisbury honoured in this way and, during her term of office, proved to be an enthusiastic and dedicated mayor.

Edith Hulse, wife of the MP for Salisbury, devoted much of her life to the welfare of the people of that city. Deeply interested in education, she served on the Board of Governors for several local schools, but her greatest contribution, perhaps, was the provision and endowment of 'a commodious and well-equipped Maternity and Child Welfare Clinic at Salisbury Infirmary'.

HONORA JACKSON

1867–1950
(née Butson)
Lived: Longcroft House, Devizes

For many years it has not been possible to think of art in Devizes without Mrs Jackson's name coming at once to mind. (*Wiltshire Gazette* obituary, August 1950)

At a time when it was not considered at all respectable, Honora Butson persuaded her parents to allow her to study art in both London and Paris. Her persistence was justified when some of her work was exhibited at the Royal Academy in London. In the 1890s she started to paint portraits in oils and several well-known people sat for her,

including the actress, Mrs Patrick Campbell.

After her marriage to a solicitor, Mr Guy Jackson, of Devizes, Wiltshire, and the birth of a daughter, Honora continued to work. She painted the countryside around Devizes in water-colours, she painted portraits of local dignitaries and, during the 1939–45 war, she renovated the portraits in the Assembly Room of the Devizes Town Hall. Her most interesting commission, perhaps, was to paint many of the inn-signs in the district.

EGLANTYNE JEBB

1876–1928
St Peter's Church,
Marlborough

If we are not prepared to save these children, if we can harden our hearts against their sufferings, if we can remain indifferent to our most elementary human obligations towards them, what manner of people are we? ('Save the Child', a posthumous essay by Eglantyne Jebb, 1929)

Eglantyne Jebb was the founder of the Save the Children Fund. Born in Shropshire, she read History at Oxford and then trained to be a teacher at Stockwell Training College, London. Her first post was as assistant teacher at St Peter's Church School, Marlborough, in Wiltshire, and it was there in 1899 that she encountered for the first time the problems of children from poor families.

Moving to Cambridge, Eglantyne became a member of the Cambridge Education Committee.

In 1912 war broke out in the Balkans and she went there to help with relief work. Her experiences of the sufferings of refugees, particularly the children, throughout the First World War, made her passionately determined to bring the issue to public notice.

In 1919 Eglantyne Jebb started Save the Children Fund. Eventually the movement spread into forty countries and contributions to the Fund reached five and a half million pounds. She drew up a Charter of Children's Rights and took it to the League of Nations. The Charter was brought forward in 1924 and much of it was incorporated into the 'Declaration of the Rights of the Child' (Children's Charter).

Eglantyne Jebb died in Geneva in 1928. She was only fifty-two.

CONSTANCE KENT

1844–1944?
St Thomas à Becket Church, Coulston

The church of St Thomas à Becket at Coulston, Wiltshire, is surrounded by trees. In the churchyard lies a large, rather sombre slab marking the burial place of a woman and a small boy, both named Kent. The little boy was the victim in one of the most controversial murders ever recorded and the inscription, now almost indecipherable, once read:

> Mary Anne Saville Kent, who died May 5, 1852, aged 44, and Francis Saville Kent, who was cruelly murdered at Rode, June 30th, 1860, aged three years and ten months – shall not God search this out, for He knoweth the secrets of the heart.

The 'secrets of the heart' have baffled writers ever since, for, although little Francis Kent's half-sister, Constance, eventually confessed to the horrific murder, very few people believed that she was actually guilty.

Constance Kent was born at Sidmouth in Devon, the ninth child of Samuel Kent and his wife, Mary Anne. Later, the family moved to Somerset and then to East

Coulston, Wiltshire, by which time they had acquired a lively and pretty governess called Mary Pratt Mr Kent, it was rumoured, was infatuated with Mary.

Mrs Kent gave birth to her tenth child, William, and her husband moved into a separate room. Gradually Mrs Kent was left more and more in the seclusion of her bedroom and Mary Pratt took over the running of the household. Then suddenly, Mrs Kent died. Just over a year later Mr Kent married Mary Pratt. Constance was almost nine years old.

At first Constance and her new stepmother seemed to get on well but the relationship began to deteriorate. Constance became ill and was sent to Bath for medical treatment, boarding at a school there. When she came home for the summer holidays, the second Mrs Kent treated her so harshly that she ran away with her younger brother. They were soon discovered by the police and sent home, both were punished and Constance was sent away again.

The second Mrs Kent gave birth to a son, christened Francis, and when, in 1859, Constance came home, she seemed to be very fond of her little stepbrother. A young woman, Elizabeth Gough, was employed as a nurse and, once again, it was rumoured that Mr Kent found her very attractive.

Then, one night in June 1860, the whole family went to bed as usual. The next morning, Francis was missing from his cot.

His body was eventually discovered in the garden privy – he had been suffocated, violently stabbed and his throat had been cut, almost severing his head from his body. When, in July, Constance was arrested, held in Devizes gaol and charged with murder, both public and press reacted with stunned disbelief. Local opinion turned against Mr Kent and the atmosphere became unpleasant. In August, Constance was sent home again and, in September, Elizabeth Gough was arrested. She, too, was released.

In 1864, when the whole affair had almost been forgotten,

Constance, who was being prepared for confirmation, suddenly confessed to the murder. No one seems to have believed her, but she insisted she was guilty and was held at Devizes and then moved to Salisbury. At the Assizes, in an atmosphere of the most profound emotion, she was condemned to death for the murder of her stepbrother. The sentence was later commuted to penal servitude. Constance remained in various prisons for twenty years and was released in 1885. She then disappeared.

Yseult Bridges in her book *Saint – With Red Hands?* (1954) leaves one with the strong impression that Constance Kent did *not* commit the murder. Bernard Taylor, on the other hand, in *Cruelly Murdered* (1979) seems quite convinced that she *did*. He also claims that Constance emigrated to Australia, trained as a nurse there under the name of Ruth Emilie Kaye, and died at Strathfield, New South Wales, in 1944.

Slab grave of Constance Kent's step brother, Francis Saville Kent, in the churchyard of St Thomas à Becket, Coulston

COLLEGE OF MATRONS

Founded 1682

Salisbury Close

As one walks through the main gateway into Salisbury Cathedral Close, the first building one notices is on the left: it is long, low and has an air of warmth and dignity most suitable for a College of Matrons.

The story behind the founding of the college is delightfully romantic. Seth Ward, Bishop of Salisbury from 1667–1689, is said to have fallen in love as a young man, but the woman of his choice refused

him and instead married a clergyman of Exeter.

Many years later her husband died and she was left almost destitute. Bishop Seth Ward, hearing of her plight, promptly founded the College of Matrons, a home for twelve poor widows of clergymen in the dioceses of Salisbury and Exeter. The building has been used for the same purpose ever since.

CHARLOTTE ANNE ELIZABETH (ANNIE) MOBERLY

1846–1937
Lived: Bishop's Palace, Salisbury

Annie Moberly was born in Winchester in 1846, the tenth of fifteen children of George Moberly, headmaster of Winchester School, and his wife Mary Ann. Annie was twenty when her father became Bishop of Salisbury and the family moved to the Bishop's Palace there. For another twenty years she read, played the piano and acted as her father's secretary and nurse–companion. In 1886, after her father's death, Annie went to Oxford and took charge of St Hugh's, a new hall for women students. In 1901 she visited Paris and stayed there with her friend, Eleanor Jourdain:

After some days of sight-seeing in Paris . . . on an August afternoon, 1901, Miss Jourdain and I went to Versailles. We had very hazy ideas as to where it was or what there was to be seen. Both of us thought it might prove to be a dull expedition. (*An Adventure*, Miss Morison and Miss Lamont – Miss Moberly and Miss Jourdain, 1911)

'A dull expedition' was the last thing their visit proved to be. After seeing the palace, they decided to take a walk in the grounds towards the Petit Trianon:

From the moment we left the lane an extraordinary depression had come over me, which, in spite of every effort to shake off, steadily deepened . . . Everything suddenly looked unnatural, therefore unpleasant, even the trees behind the building seemed to have become flat and lifeless, like a wood worked in tapestry.

Both Annie and Eleanor saw, heard and even spoke to, various people in strange costume – all of whom behaved in a slightly odd manner. The two women did not discuss their experience until much later. Then, convinced that they had witnessed events connected with the French Revolution in 1789, they began the long research which culminated in a book called *An Adventure*, first published in 1911.

An Adventure provoked great interest – and even greater controversy. Did Annie Moberly and her friend Eleanor Jourdain *really* see the ghosts of Marie Antoinette, the Comte de Vaudreuil and others? Why should someone like Annie Moberly have lied? The mystery is as fresh and fascinating as ever.

EDITH OLIVIER

1879–1948
Lived: The Daye House, Wilton

No one could have been better qualified to write about Wiltshire than Edith Olivier. Born in the Rectory at Wilton, near Salisbury, she was educated at home and then at Oxford. During the 1914–18 war she was an officer in the Women's Land Army in Wiltshire, and it was not until 1927, when she was forty-eight, that her first book was published:

I woke up in the middle of the night with the idea of a story in my head. I had not thought of it before that moment, but it struck me as being a very good subject, and I immediately sat up and scribbled away for three or four hours . . . Before morning I had finished two chapters of 'The Love Child' – my first book. (Edith Olivier, *Without Knowing Mr Walkley*, 1938)

Then came a spate of novels, *Moonrakings*, a collection of short stories, and in 1938 *Without Knowing Mr Walkley: Personal Memories*.

It was in this book that Edith Olivier's gift for writing about people really blossomed. With a wicked sense of humour and with great affection she described people she had known, from Lady Pembroke and the (very deaf) Parish Nurse, to Miss Young, the local postmistress, who 'seemed to be overcome with rage if anyone dared to buy a stamp from her'.

Edith Olivier was the Mayor of Wilton from 1938–1941. She continued to write and, not long before her death, published *Four Victorian Ladies of Wiltshire*, which included Annie Moberly (q.v.) and Barbara Townsend (q.v.). Wiltshire.

MARY HERBERT, COUNTESS OF PEMBROKE

1561–1621
(née Sidney)

Lived: Wilton House, Wilton, near Salisbury

She was a beautiful Ladie and had an excellent witt, and had the best breeding that that age could afford. Shee had a pritty sharpe-ovall face. Her haire was of a reddish yellowe. (John Aubrey's *Brief Lives*, 1813)

Mary Sidney married Henry, second Earl of Pembroke, in 1577 and became the mistress of Wilton House, near Salisbury in Wiltshire. It was at Wilton that she entertained many of the great minds of that dazzling age – including William Shakespeare. It was here too that she studied chemistry, wrote poetry, worked on translations and, it is said, suggested the composition of *The Arcadia* to her brother, Sir Philip Sidney. Among others, she knew and helped Ben Johnson, Philip Massinger, John Donne, Thomas Nashe and Nicholas Breton.

At Wilton House, described by John Aubrey as 'an Arcadian plac and a Paradise', it is quite easy to imagine the Countess of Pembrok walking by the river with her brother, talking to her guests, or gazing from a window as she wrote.

Mary Herbert was sadly misse and sincerely mourned when she died. She was buried in the Pembroke vault in Salisbury Cathedral.

Wilton House

RUTH PIERCE

d. 1753

Market Cross, Devizes

The market cross in Devizes, Wiltshire, is, rather sadly, usually surrounded by parked cars. It is, however, worth a close inspection as it bears a long and very unusual inscription:

The mayor and corporation of Devizes avail themselves of the stability of this building to transmit to future times the record of an awful event which occurred in this market place, in the year 1753 . . . On Thursday, 25th January 1753, Ruth Pierce of Potterne in this county, agreed with three other women to buy a sack of wheat in the market each paying her due proportion towards the same; one of these

women in collecting the several quotas of money, discovered a deficiency and demanded of Ruth Pierce the sum which was wanting to make good the amount; Ruth Pierce protested that she had paid her share and wished she might drop down dead if she had not. She rashly repeated this awful wish, when to the consternation and terror of the surrounding multitude, she instantly fell down and expired, having the money concealed in her hand.

Poor Ruth Pierce! At the inquest the jury declared that she had been struck dead with a lie in her mouth, by the visitation of the Great and Almighty God.

Market Cross, Devizes

CATHERINE, DUCHESS OF QUEENSBERRY

1701–1777
(née Hyde)
Lived: Amesbury Abbey,
Amesbury

When she was young, the Duchess of Queensberry was admired because she was very beautiful, intelligent and lively. As she grew older she continued to be admired for the same reasons – but was also enjoyed for her eccentricities. She knew, among others, Matthew Prior, Dean Swift, Horace Walpole and Alexander Pope, and was the patroness of John Gay, author of *The Beggar's Opera* (1728). One of her several homes was at Amesbury, in Wiltshire.

Catherine married Charles Douglas, third Duke of Queensberry in 1720. She gave birth to two sons and a daughter.

The Queensberrys first met John Gay in Bath. When *Polly* (his sequel to the successful *Beggar's Opera*) was refused a licence for its performance, the Duchess came to the rescue and began to collect subscriptions for its publication. As a result she was banned from Court. *Polly* was a huge success

and John Gay became secretary to the Queensberrys.

As she grew older, Catherine began to develop a delightful dottiness. Her clothes became distinctly odd and so, at times, did her behaviour. She once drove from London to a friend's house in Parsons Green and arrived saying she had something of great importance to tell her. When asked what the urgent message was, she said 'Why, take a couple of beefsteaks, clap them together, as if they were for a dumpling, and eat them with pepper and salt; it is the best thing you ever tasted.' She then departed at great speed.

Catherine, Duchess of Queensberry, died in London. She once wrote to a friend:

Adieu, my dear Lady Suffolk, and good night. I must go to bed in order to get up again, most creatures are made for nothing else, but only they don't know it and I do.

ANN RAXWORTHY

1747–1829
Buried: St John the
Baptist Church, Stockton

Beneath one's feet as one steps into the porch of the church in Stockton, Wiltshire, there is a large, flat gravestone. It is unusual to find a grave in such a position, but the choice was deliberate, and the reason oddly moving.

Ann Raxworthy was a lady's maid and, when she retired from her work, she was allowed to live in a cottage called Diana's, next to the church. Whenever Ann attended a service there she wore her best black silk gown, and it was this minor vanity that began to trouble her conscience. Worried that her black silk had been a sign of too much pride, Ann requested that when she died she should be buried where everyone would walk over her.

GRACE REED

Nineteenth century

The Royal Oak's inn sign,
Great Wishford

For centuries the villagers of Wishford and Barford St Martin in Wiltshire had the right to gather dry wood from Grovely Forest. They were also allowed to gather a load of young oak trees, which they used to decorate their homes and their churches. Once this was done the villagers took the remaining branches to Salisbury Cathedral, where they offered them up before the high altar, chanting 'Grovely! Grovely! and all Grovely!', then they danced in the Cathedral Close.

All this happened on 29 May – Oak Apple Day – and, thanks to Grace Reed, of Barford, the tradition continues to this day.

Grovely Forest is part of the estate owned by the Earls of Pembroke, granted to them by Henry VIII. In the nineteenth century, following the Enclosure Acts, one of the Earls tried to put an end to the villagers' wood-gathering rights. Grace Reed and three of her friends decided to defy the ban and went out to gather wood on the appropriate day. The four women were summoned before the magistrates, but refused to pay the fine and were promptly imprisoned. They were released the next day . . . the Earl had changed his mind.

DORA ROBERTSON

1893–1972
(née Butterworth)
Salisbury Close, Salisbury

After being an ambulance and War Office driver during the war, I had, in 1920, taken a course at King's College for Women, with the idea of applying American methods of labour saving, in which I was interested, to household work. (Dora Robertson, *Sarum Close*, 1938)

Dora Butterworth, after the course at King's College, London, was offered a post as school matron at the Salisbury Cathedral Choristers School in 1925. She accepted, but after only three months there fell in love with the headmaster, Canon A. G. Robertson. They were married the same year.

Dora helped her husband to run the school until his retirement. In 1938 her book, *Sarum Close: A*

History of the Life and Education of the Cathedral Choristers was published.

She admitted herself that her book had overstepped the bounds of her original intention:

This book started life as the history of these boys. It has grown into something more complex, and has become as research brought more and more details to light, a picture of the domestic life of a whole community over those seven hundred years. This community lives inside a wall and the gates are locked at night.

Dora Robertson became a much-valued member of that community. She died there in 1972.

ELA, COUNTESS OF SALISBURY

c. 1187–1261
Buried: Lacock Abbey

Ela was a woman of great public spirit. She obtained for the Lacock people the right to hold a market every Tuesday, and also a three-days' fair at St. Thomas-tide. (Matilda Talbot (q.v.), *My Life and Lacock Abbey*, 1956)

In 1198 Ela was married to William Longespée (Longsword), the stepbrother of Richard I, the Lion Heart. She was twelve years old. Ela is said to have given birth to four sons and four daughters. When her husband died in 1226,

she built a house for monks at her manor in Somerset and called it Locus Dei. A little later she founded the abbey at Lacock in Wiltshire, for nuns of the order of St Augustine and there, in 1238, she herself took the veil. A year later she was elected Abbess, a position she held until she resigned through ill health. She was buried in the beautiful abbey she had founded.

The cloisters of Lacock Abbey

MARY SANDALL

fl. 1779
Lived: Baverstock

A Baverstock woman 'of about twenty-four years of age, of middle stature, and by no means of a masculine aspect'. (Edith Olivier, *Wiltshire*, 1951)

There have been many highwaymen, but very few highwaywomen. Mary Sandall was one of the exceptions. Unfortunately, little is known about Mary's life, and even less about why she attempted her inept and amateurish hold-up.

Whatever the reason, in 1779 a Mrs Thring, who lived near Wilton, was walking home when a person on horseback drew up, produced a pistol, and demanded her money. Poor Mrs Thring surrendered two shillings and her silk cloak, but when the highwayman demanded not only her ring but her shoe-buckles, she pretended that she could see her husband in the distance. The highwayman galloped off.

Mrs Thring hurried home, raised the alarm, and the thief was soon caught. To everyone's astonishment, the highwayman was not only a *woman*, but was quite well-known to everyone in the district. She was indicted by the name of Mary Abraham (alias Mary Sandall) and sentenced to death, but later reprieved.

JANE SEYMOUR

1509?–1537
Lived: Wolf Hall (no longer exists), Burbage

Queen Jane lay in labour full nine
    days or more,
Till the women were so tired, they
    could stay no longer there,
Till the women were so tired, they
    could stay no longer there.

The Queen referred to in the old English ballad, *The Death of Queen Jane*, was Jane Seymour, Henry VIII's third wife. She was one of the Seymours of Savernake, whose home was at Wolf Hall, Burbage in Wiltshire, and it was there, so the story goes, that the King first met and courted her.

On 19 May 1536, Henry VIII's second wife, Anne Boleyn, was executed at the tower of London.

On 30 May, the King married Jane Seymour in the Queen's Chapel at Whitehall. About a year later, on Trinity Sunday, 1537, a *Te Deum* was sung at St Paul's Cathedral, to celebrate the new Queen's 'quickening of child', and in October that year Jane gave birth to a son at Hampton Court Palace. Twelve days later she died. They buried her in St George's Chapel, Windsor.

And how deep was the mourning,
    how black were the bands,
How yellow, yellow were the
    flamboys they carried in their
    hands.

DR ELSIE SMITH, PH.D., BA

1891–1977
Salisbury Cathedral Library

During the present century one person who seemed to know more about Salisbury Cathedral and its priceless treasures than any other living soul was the Librarian, Dr Elsie Smith. (Pamela Street, *Portrait of Wiltshire*, 1971)

Born at Dartford, Kent, Dr Elsie Smith taught for sixteen years there before moving to Salisbury in 1927. She then lectured at Salisbury Diocesan Training College (now the College of Sarum St Michael) and later became head of the English Department. From the beginning she showed a passionate interest in the cathedral, and particularly the cathedral library.

In 1943 she was appointed Assistant Librarian and in 1953 she became Cathedral Librarian. Apart from opening the library to visitors, she not only trained voluntary helpers as guides but accumulated all the admission fees, which were then used to buy books and manuscripts for the collection.

Dr Elsie Smith died in 1977, having spent over forty years of her life working in the Salisbury Cathedral Library.

MATILDA TALBOT

1871–1958
(née Gilchrist-Clark)
Lacock and Lacock Abbey

Lacock Abbey has always been ready to adopt the role of a chameleon and change its colour as required. I remember in my uncle's time, when life was necessarily sometimes very quiet I used to feel that the house didn't really want to be so quiet, but would like to have a party. (Matilda Talbot, *My Life and Lacock Abbey*, 1956)

Matilda Gilchrist-Clark, born in Dumfriesshire, Scotland, led a fairly ordinary life. Educated in London and trained as a cookery teacher, she was known to her friends as Maudie.

During the 1914–18 war Matilda was involved with the Red Cross in France, and also became commander of the WRNS (Women's Royal Naval Service) at Cranwell in Lincolnshire. Her whole life changed suddenly and unexpectedly when her uncle, Charles Talbot, the owner of Lacock, near Chippenham in Wiltshire, died in December 1916:

Two days later, when the quiet funeral was over, the lawyer returned with us to the house and we went into the library, where he read us the will. The whole situation was rather like a scene in an old-fashioned novel. My uncle had left everything he possessed to me, without trustees or conditions of any kind.

Matilda, with remarkable poise, assumed the name of Talbot by deed poll and took over the responsibilities of Lacock Abbey, a village of about eight hundred inhabitants, and an original copy of Henry III's confirmation of the Magna Carta. For nearly thirty years she lived and entertained there, receiving a London Elementary School and several units of troops during the Second World War.

In 1944 she presented Lacock Abbey, village and Manor Farm to the National Trust, and gave the Magna Carta to the British Museum. Remaining there as a tenant, Matilda Talbot died in 1958 and was buried in the village cemetery.

OLIVE TALBOT

d. 1651?
(née Sharington)
The Sharington Tower, Lacock Abbey

Olive, the daughter of Sir Henry Sharington, owner of Lacock Abbey in Wiltshire, fell in love with John Talbot, brother of the Earl of Shrewsbury. Her father strongly opposed the match – as fathers will – which only made the young man more attractive. Olive continued to see him – as daughters will.

One night, talking to her lover from the window of a tower at her home, Olive, carried away by the romance of the situation, suggested that she should jump down to him. According to John Aubrey in his *Brief Lives*, young John Talbot, not for a moment believing that she would do such a thing laughingly said he would catch her. Olive jumped.

Although the wind, catching her skirts, slowed down her progress, she nevertheless knocked her suitor unconscious and, quite convinced that he was dead, she screamed for help. When young Talbot eventually came round, Olive's father, rather crisply, told her that 'since she had made such a leap she should e'en marrie him', and so she did.

Nothing else in her life ever equalled such excitement. When John Talbot died, Olive married Sir Robert Stapelton, who came from Yorkshire, and when he died she lived on at Lacock.

Opposite: **Olive Talbot jumped from a tower at Lacock Abbey**

PAMELA GENEVIEVE ADELAIDE TENNANT (LADY GLENCONNER)

1871–1928
(née Wyndham)
Lived: Clouds, East Knoyle

In the valley of the Wylye the little villages edge the banks of the river at a distance of about a mile from each other.
They are built in squares of flint and stone, and the thatched roofs are, in parts, golden with yellow stonecrop. (Pamela Tennant, *Village Notes*, 1900)

Pamela Tennant was the youngest daughter of the Hon. Percy Scawen Wyndham of Clouds, East Knoyle, Wiltshire. She married Edward Tennant, later Baron Glenconner, in 1895, and they lived for some time at Stockton Manor. Pamela Tennant began to write descriptive essays about the area and the people who lived there. They were published together as *Village Notes*. Pamela Tennant continued to write, producing articles for magazines and a 'Book of Verse with Legends in Rhyme' called *Windelstraw*. Her eldest son was killed in France in 1916 and, three years later, her *Edward Wyndham Tennant. A Memoir by his Mother*, was published. She dedicated it to:

All those Mothers who have suffered the same loss. They will forgive the imperfections, and all I have found good to tell of my son here, they will feel to be most true of theirs.

Lady Glenconner moved to Wilsford Manor near Devizes. She had inherited a great interest in Spiritualism from her father and, after her husband's death, she published *The Earthen Vessel. A Volume dealing with Spirit Communications received in the form of Book Tests* (1921). After her second marriage, to Viscount Grey of Fallodon, she continued to live much of the time at Wilsford Manor. Spiritualism became more and more important to her and in an appreciation in *The Times* after her death, a friend, Sir Oliver Lodge, said:

Throughout her later life the subject dominated her thoughts, she was consulted by many people in distress and on the strength of truly remarkable evidence she attained profound conviction of immortality.

HELEN BERENICE THOMAS

1877–1967
(née Noble)
Lived: Starwell Farm near Chippenham

Mrs Helen Thomas, who died on Wednesday . . . was the widow of the poet Edward Thomas, who was killed in Flanders on Easter Monday, April 9, 1917: thus she died three days after the 50th anniversary of his death. (*Times* obituary, 1967)

Nine years after her husband's death, Helen Thomas wrote the story of their life together, from the time they first met to the birth of their son Mervyn in 1900. The book called *As It Was* (1926) was short, painfully honest and controversial. Some critics took exception to the fact that she described the first time that they had made love together:

Then, keeping his eyes fixed so tenderly and seriously and passionately on mine, he undid my dress and took my arms out of the sleeves, and unfastened my underclothes.

When interviewed by the *Evening Standard*, Helen Thomas 'appeared rather surprised that any explanation of how so simple a study came to be published should be sought'. In 1931 she published a sequel, called *World Without End*.
Helen lived very happily for almost twenty years at Starwell Farm, near Chippenham, in Wiltshire. She later moved to Berkshire and wrote from there:

The aconites – a special favourite of mine – I can't get to do well here. At my farm in Wiltshire, which I wish you'd seen, they spread and flowered directly after Christmas . . . But it was a most lovely land for flowers. I miss most deeply the rich hedgebanks full of primroses and violets and cowslips.

BARBARA TOWNSEND

1842–1939
Lived: Mompesson
House, Salisbury Close

A small trim figure, with a resolute gait, she walked about, swathed in cloaks, capes, shawls, scarves, and veils, superimposed one over the other, and falling behind her in graceful disarray. Her features were small and finely cut, her mouth firm, her eyes intent. She had a quiet voice, and spoke distinctly. (Edith Olivier, *Four Victorian Ladies of Wiltshire*, 1945)

Barbara Townsend, described in her later years so delightfully by Edith Olivier (q.v.), was born in Salisbury and lived most of her long life in Mompesson House in the Cathedral Close. She was a very gifted amateur artist, mostly in water-colour, although she painted some oils and also enjoyed painting on china. Working almost

entirely for her own pleasure and satisfaction, her output was prodigious, resulting in a unique record of her life, her surroundings, and the people and places that she loved.

Until recently none of her work had been seen outside her family, but in 1984 a small exhibition was staged by the National Trust at Mompesson House (now a Trust property). Interest and enthusiasm was such that a second exhibition followed a year later.

Barbara Townsend was buried in the Cloister of Salisbury Cathedral. She is spoken of by those who knew her with great warmth, affection and admiration.

Mompesson House

HANNAH TWYNNOY

1670–1703
Buried: Malmesbury
Abbey Churchyard

In October 1703, a travelling menagerie set up its tents and cages in the town of Malmesbury in Wiltshire, and people came from miles around to gaze and gasp at the wild animals.

Unfortunately a tiger escaped from its cage one day and poor Hannah Twynnoy, who worked locally, happened to be in the wrong place at very much the wrong time. She was so severely mauled that she died of her wounds.

Hannah was buried in Malmesbury Abbey churchyard and the dramatic circumstances of her tragic death, combined with an unusual epitaph, have ensured the regular restoration of her gravestone. The words on it are as clear today as they were nearly three hundred years ago.

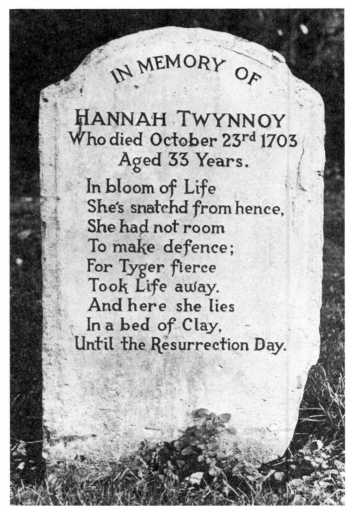

IN MEMORY OF
HANNAH TWYNNOY
Who died October 23ʳᵈ 1703
Aged 33 Years.

In bloom of Life
She's snatchd from hence,
She had not room
To make defence;
For Tyger fierce
Took Life away.
And here she lies
In a bed of Clay,
Until the Resurrection Day.

ELEANOR WARRE

fl. 1905
St John's Church,
Bemerton, near Salisbury

A brief sentence in Pevsner's *Wiltshire* referring to a 'handsome mosaic and gesso frieze . . . designed and made by Miss Nellie Warre', led us to St John's Church at Bemerton.

In spite of various enquiries, Eleanor Warre remains an enigma. All that is known is that she was one of the daughters of the Rector of St John's, Canon Francis Warre, and his wife, Mary Caroline.

Although her father, mother and a sister, Pauline, are all buried in the churchyard, Eleanor herself has disappeared, leaving only her work to be admired.

LADY LOUISA,
VISCOUNTESS
WEYMOUTH
1713–1736
(née Granville)
Lived: Longleat House
near Warminster

Longleat House

A corridor on the top floor of Longleat House, Wiltshire, is said to be haunted by the ghost of Louisa, the second wife of Thomas Thynne, second Viscount Weymouth. The legend is that Lord Weymouth fought a duel along this corridor with an unknown man, who was supposed to be his wife's lover, and killed him. He then buried the body at Longleat:

> It is possible that this terrible story is true. When central heating was put into Longleat, during the Fifth Marquess's lifetime, the body of a man was found buried in the cellars. He was wearing jackboots, which crumbled away as soon as the body was exposed to the air. (Daphne Bath, *Longleat*, 1949)

However, in the records of Louisa's brief life there is no evidence that such an incident occurred. She married Lord Weymouth in 1733 when she was nineteen. They lived at Longleat but spent part of each year at their London house. In 1734 Louisa gave birth to a son and a year later

to a second. By the summer of 1736 she was pregnant again and in December that year gave birth to another boy. It was a difficult birth and she fell dangerously ill. Mrs Delany, a close friend, was staying there at the time. She wrote to her sister:

> My Lady Weymouth continues extremely ill . . . her fever is very high, and she has been the greater part of that time delirious: she has had *nine* blisters, but to *no purpose but to torment her*, for they have *injured her much*! So melancholy a house I never saw.

Before she had finished the letter, Mrs Delany added this sad sentence: '*Poor dear Lady Weymouth is gone; she died at half an hour after five.*'

Louisa died aged twenty-three. She was buried in the family vault at Longbridge Deverill. A few days later Mrs Delany wrote again to her sister:

> As to my Lord, he will console himself, for he is a man, and one who is more subject to joy than grief.

EMILY HILDA YOUNG

1880–1949
(Mrs Daniell)
Lived: Bradford-on-Avon

A novelist of rare quality, possessed of a singular clarity of imaginative sympathy with the springs of normal character and experience, she stood aside from the tendency of most of her contemporaries. It might be thought sentimental nowadays, so self-conscious have we become where the enduring commonplaces of life are concerned, to say of her as a novelist that she saw life steadily and saw it whole. (*Times* obituary, 1949)

Emily Young, better known later as E. H. Young, was born in Northumberland, the daughter of a ship owner. Educated at Gateshead High School and Penrhos College, Colwyn Bay, Wales, she studied philosophy and logic. In 1902 she married a solicitor, J. A. H. Daniell, and moved to Bristol. It was there that she wrote her first novel, *A Corn of Wheat* (1910).

In 1917, during the First World War, her husband was killed at Ypres. E. H. Young moved to London, where she met and fell in love with Ralph Henderson, headmaster of Alleyn's School in Dulwich:

She did not live alone; neither did she ever remarry. Rather, in circumstances quite extraordinary for the period, she lived with a married man, ostensibly in a separate flat, in the same house as his wife. (Introduction by Sally Beauman to 1984 Virago edition of *The Misses Mallett*)

During this period of her life, E. H. Young wrote several novels, including her very successful *William* (1925) and *Miss Mole* (1930), for which she won the James Tait Black Memorial Prize.

When Ralph Henderson retired in 1940, he and E. H. Young moved to Bradford-on-Avon in Wiltshire. It was here that she wrote two children's books and her last novel, *Chatterton Square* (1947).

ALPHABETICAL INDEX: WITH COUNTIES

Also of interest

IN OUR GRANDMOTHER'S FOOTSTEPS
A Virago Guide to London
JENNIFER CLARKE
Photographs by Joanna Parkin

This informative, witty and beautifully illustrated guide is both a gazetteer and a fascinating recognition of women's accomplishments throughout history. The procession of our foremothers is one of infinite variety: hidden away in London's corners are memorials to women who were writers, mystics, gardeners, suffragettes, cooks, composers, mistresses and masqueraders as men, pickpockets and murderers. Here are the famous, the infamous, and the unknown – from the great tragic actress Sarah Siddons to the daunting Miss Beale, from the energetic Mrs Beeton to the militant Ann Kenney.

Pursuing endless clues, Jennifer Clarke and Joanna Parkin have unearthed statues in quiet corners of museums, portraits in galleries, memorials tucked away in churches, and graves in sprawling cemeteries. To help in locating these sites is a separate listing, taking London area by area, of the memorial to the more than 270 women included here. This listing is arranged so that walkers can follow easily in our grandmothers' footsteps.

VIRAGO TRAVELLERS

Lady Barker
STATION LIFE IN NEW
   ZEALAND

Gertrude Bell
THE DESERT AND THE SOWN

Isabella Bird
A LADY'S LIFE IN THE
   ROCKY MOUNTAINS
UNBEATEN TRACKS IN
   JAPAN
THE YANGTZE VALLEY AND
   BEYOND

Dora Birtles
NORTH-WEST BY NORTH

Mildred Cable
THE GOBI DESERT

Alexandra David-Neel
MY JOURNEY TO LHASA

Edith Durham
HIGH ALBANIA

Isabelle Eberhardt
Translated by Nina de Voogd
THE PASSIONATE NOMAD

Emily Eden
UP THE COUNTRY

Amelia Edwards
UNTRODDEN PEAKS AND
   UNFREQUENTED VALLEYS

Lucie Duff Gordon
LETTERS FROM EGYPT

Emily Hahn
CHINA TO ME

Mary Kingsley
TRAVELS IN WEST AFRICA

Ella K. Maillart
THE CRUEL WAY

Beryl Markham
WEST WITH THE NIGHT

Susanna Moodie
ROUGHING IT IN THE BUSH

Kate O'Brien
FAREWELL SPAIN

Flora Tristan
Translated by Jean Hawkes
THE LONDON JOURNAL OF
   FLORA TRISTAN
PEREGRINATIONS OF A
   PARIAH

WOMEN PHOTOGRAPHERS
The Other Observers 1900 to the Present
Val Williams

In this fascinating view of British women photographers, obscured by time,
fashion and the mere fact of being the 'other observers', Val Williams charts
their course from the turn of the century to the 1980s. The early documentar
work by the 'Women of Pervyse' of the First World War and Norah Smyth's
photographs of London's East End are in sharp contrast to Christina Broom
glamorous and flamboyant suffrage portraits. From the 1920s to the '50s
Vanessa Bell created the Charleston idyll of family life in her seemingly casu
snapshots. Counterposed to this domesticity was the innovative and modish
photography of Barbara Ker-Seymer and Ursula Powys-Lybbe. Different
again in approach and concerns was the radical documentary work of Helen
Muspratt and Edith Tudor Hart, and Grace Robertson's photojournalism fc
Picture Post, while the surrealist imaginings of Madame Yevonde carry
studio portraiture in quite new directions. Val Williams persuasively
demonstrates how this richly diverse inheritance reflects itself in today's ran
of approaches: from community-based photography to photomontage, fron
the celebratory pictures of women at Greenham Common to questioning
looks at self-image. *Women Photographers* is an original and invaluable
addition to photographic and cultural history.

A VERY GREAT PROFESSION
The Woman's Novel 1914–39
Nicola Beauman

'Katharine, thus, was a member of a very great profession which has, as yet, no title and very little recognition . . . She lived at home.'
— *Virginia Woolf, Night and Day*

In this book, Nicola Beauman looks at women like Katharine, women whose circumstances are generally ignored by social historians, but whose lives and habits are wonderfully recorded in the fiction of the time. Drawing on the novels to illuminate domestic life, romantic love, sex, psychoanalysis, war and 'surplus' women, Nicola Beauman uses the work of such diverse women novelists as May Sinclair and Elinor Glyn, Rebecca West and E. M. Delafield, Rosamond Lehmann and Mary Borden – and many, many more – to present a fascinating portrait, through fiction, of middle-class Englishwomen between the wars.

'Wonderfully researched and well written. Nicola Beauman's analysis is infinitely sharp, subtle and entertaining' – Molly Keane, *The Irish Times*

'Sympathetic, affectionate . . . an excellent tribute' – Penelope Mortimer, *Sunday Telegraph*